RETENTION OF TITLE ON THE SALE OF GOODS

JOHN PARRIS
LLB(Hons), PhD

GRANADA
London Toronto Sydney New York

Granada Publishing Limited – Technical Books Division
Frogmore, St Albans, Herts AL2 2NF
and
36 Golden Square, London W1R 4AH
866 United Nations Plaza, New York, NY 10017, USA
117 York Street, Sydney, NSW 2000, Australia
100 Skyway Avenue, Rexdale, Ontario, Canada M9W 3A6
61 Beach Road, Auckland, New Zealand

British Library Cataloguing in Publication Data
    Parris, John
        Retention of title of the sale of goods
        1. Commercial law – Great Britain
        I. Title
        344.106'72 KD1650

ISBN 0 246 11612 9

First published in Great Britain 1982 by Granada Publishing

Printed in Great Britain by Richard Clay (The Chaucer Press) Ltd,
Bungay, Suffolk

Granada ®
Granada Publishing ®

Contents

Preface

This is not a book written for lawyers, although it may profitably be read by them. It is written primarily for businessmen who are tired of supplying goods on credit to companies, only to find these goods seized without payment by a receiver for some secured creditor, usually a bank.

In the *Bond Worth* case, for example, some £550,000 of Acrilan supplied by Monsanto, and on hand in various forms on the carpet manufacturer's premises, was utilised to satisfy the claims of the debenture holders, Alliance Assurance Co. Ltd.

With Lord Justice Templeman, I believe that unsecured creditors receive a raw deal.

This does not therefore claim to be an impartial book. In fact, it is a partisan book. It is written to advise manufacturers and suppliers of goods how they can protect themselves against receivers and liquidators.

Regrettably, two decisions of the courts have swung the balance very much in favour of secured creditors. Accepting these decisions for the time being, as we must, this book is designed to indicate to businessmen what retention of title clauses should prove effective even in the light of these decisions.

I am deeply grateful to Professor R.R. Pennington, LLB, LLD, Solicitor, Dean of the Faculty of Law at the University of Birmingham, author of *Pennington's Company Law,* and sometime Special Adviser to the E.E.C., for having read the manuscript and for having made many useful suggestions. I am also indebted to him for the chapter on French, German and United States' law, which is based on an article entitled 'Retention of Title of the Sale of Goods under European Law', first published in the *International and Comparative Law Quarterly* (April 1978, pages 277-318). The article has been appropriately modified to bring it up-to-date and expanded to include United States' law.

I am also grateful to Mr F. M.B. Reynolds BCL, MA, Reader in Law at the University of Oxford; and to Mr M.J. London BSc (Econ), FCA, partner in W.H. Cork Gully & Co., for having read the script and making useful points for me to refute.

None of these gentlemen is, of course, responsible for the opinions expressed in this book — still less for my view of what the law is or should be.

Finally, I must express my thanks to Sandra den Hertog, who has wrestled with my handwriting while contending with her own offspring; and to Daniel Gerrans BA(Cantab), LLB, Barrister who is responsible for the tables of cases and statutes and for the index.

John Parris

Note

The date in parenthesis after case names is the date on which the case was first reported. Full reference is given in the table of cases at the back of the book.

Chapter 1

The Need for Retention

1.01 'A raw deal' for unsecured creditors

Shoe manufacturers supplied an old customer, a multiple retailer with a chain of shops. To their surprise, one day they saw a whole page advertisement in the local paper offering their branded goods for sale to the public through the mail at prices far below those charged to their customer. It was the first intimation they had that a receiver had been appointed to the retailers by a secured creditor, a bank.

Liquidation of the retailers followed, as is almost inevitable, and the shoe manufacturers received nothing by way of dividend for their unpaid goods; the secured creditors took all the assets. Insult was added to injury when the shoe manufacturer's markets were eroded by the sale of their branded goods to the public at less than the cost of production.

This is a not uncommon experience for manufacturers and suppliers of goods.

As Lord Justice Templeman said in the Court of Appeal in *Borden (U.K.) Ltd* v. *Scottish Timber Products Ltd and Ano.* (1979):

'Unsecured creditors rank after preferential creditors, mortgagees and holder of floating charges, and they receive a raw deal.'

He instanced the case of *Business Computers Ltd* v. *Anglo-*

African Leasing Ltd (1977) which he had tried as a High Court judge, where he said:

'The background facts are simple and depressingly typical... By commercial misfortune or administrative ineptitude B.C. Ltd lurched into insolvency and the debenture holders appointed a receiver. B.C. Ltd's assets are about £1 million. The Crown, the rating authorities and other preferential creditors take £300,000. The debenture holders take the rest; about £700,000, in part discharge of bank loans, no doubt consisting of capital and interest at the crippling rates of between 10 per cent and 20 per cent which the banks assert they are compelled to charge all and sundry. The trade creditors, who perforce extended some credit to B.C. Ltd in the ordinary course of business, and other unsecured creditors, claiming in all some £3 million, will get nothing.'

He added:

'The question whether in this day and age, it is necessary or desirable to permit the Crown and the holders of future floating charges the totality of the priorities which can be exercised under the existing law is not the subject of debate in this court, though I am inclined to think it is at least debatable elsewhere.'

Since that date, the Cork Commission on Insolvency has recommended alterations to the law which might, if adopted by Parliament, result in some crumbs being left over for unsecured creditors. But there are no signs at present that these reforms will be adopted and in any event, they would not secure unpaid suppliers payment in full for goods delivered.

1.02 'Hiving-down' operations

English law provides, as his lordship implied, a paradise for usurers. However extravagant their interest rates and however much their claim consists of unpaid interest on unpaid interest, by the term of their debentures, floating charges or secured overdrafts, they scoop the pool of assets in priority to all unsecured creditors.

The position of the latter is further prejudiced by the current practice of many receivers and liquidators, on taking possession on their appointment, of 'hiving-down' all company assets to a new and independent company. The receiver acquires an 'off the peg' £100 nominal shareholding limited liability company, registers a trading name the same or similar to that possessed by the original company, and then assigns or otherwise transfers to this new company all the assets, including goodwill, possessed by the insolvent company. The new company is thus enabled to carry on the business without the inconvenience of meeting the debts of its predecessor.

Since the unsecured creditor's only claim is against the company with whom he contracted, he is left with a claim against an empty shell from which all the crab meat has been skilfully extracted. Receivers, of course, claim that by hiving-down, it is more likely that the business will be continued and sold as a going concern, and that it is only by this method that tax losses can be preserved for the benefit of the ultimate purchaser. But this is scant comfort to unsecured creditors.

A description of an actual hiving-down operation will be found in [8.09].

1.03 Retention of title clauses
It is to seek some protection against receivers and liquidators that manufacturers and suppliers in the United Kingdom are increasingly making use of retention of title clauses in the terms and conditions in which they do business.

Such clauses have long been familiar elsewhere in Europe as *clauses de réserve de propriété, Eigentumsvorbehaltsbestimmungen* and *eigendom voorbehoudsclausulen,* and are recognised by all commercially advanced legal systems.

In its simplest form such a clause merely provides that the buyer shall not become the owner of goods until the seller has been paid.

'Unless the Company [seller] shall otherwise specify in writing, all goods sold by the Company to the purchaser shall be and remain the property of the Company until the purchase price is paid in full.

'All goods remain our property until paid for in full irrespective of any subsequent sale to a third party.'

If therefore the buyer becomes insolvent before payment, the seller is able to reclaim *his* goods from the receiver or liquidator and is not relegated to receiving a mere dividend (more often no dividend at all) years after in the insolvency of the buyer.

There is no doubt that in the United Kingdom at any time within the last three hundred years, sellers of goods could have validly imposed such a condition on their sales — always supposing, of course, that such terms were accepted by the buyers.

1.04   Conditional sales

Conditional sales of this nature (for that is all they are) have existed in English law, even before the first codification of the law relating to the sale of chattels, in the Sale of Goods Act, 1893.

Sections 17 and 19 of that Act made the position clear:

Section 17 (1): 'Where there is a contract for the sale of specific or ascertained goods, the property in them is transferred to the buyer at such time as the parties to the contract intend it to be transferred.'

Section 19 (1): 'Where there is a contract for the sale of specific goods ... the seller may, by the terms of the contract or appropriation *reserve the right of disposal of the goods until certain conditions are fulfilled.* In such cases, notwithstanding the delivery of the goods to the buyer ... the property in the goods does not pass to the buyer until the conditions imposed by the seller are fulfilled.'

From the date of the Sale of Goods Act, 1893, it was clear (as, it is submitted, it was earlier) that a seller could validly say to a buyer, 'I am not parting with ownership of these goods until you pay me, even though I allow them to pass into your possession.'

This is a simple agreement to sell subject to a condition, such as is contemplated in section 19.

1.05   Conditional sales to secure payment

Conditions of this nature were in essence recognised by the House of Lords as long ago as 1895 in *McEntire and Maconchy* v. *Crossley Brothers Ltd.* Indeed, Lord Herschell, the then Lord Chancellor, who presided, said in the course of his speech: 'I confess this appears to me to be a very plain clause.'

The appellants were the assignees in bankruptcy (as trustees in bankruptcy were then called) of one Thomas Peel, a cooper. He had on 23 June 1892 entered into a written agreement with Crossley Brothers to acquire a gas engine manufactured by them. The material parts of this agreement were:

'BETWEEN Crossley Brothers Ltd ... of Openshaw, Manchester in the County of Lancashire (hereinafter called "the owners and lessors") of the one part and Thomas Frederick Peel, cooper of 6 Cathedral Place, Limerick (hereinafter called "the lessee") of the other part.

The owners and lessors hereby agree to let to the lessee and the lessee hereby agrees to take and hire from the owners and lessors one Otto gas engine ... delivered and fixed complete in Limerick on the following conditions:—

The lessee shall and will pay to the owners and lessors as and for rent for the said 'Otto' gas engine the following sums ... which sums so agreed to be paid amount in the aggregate to the sum of £240 ... and that upon payment by the lessee of the several sums aforesaid then this agreement shall be at an end and the said Otto gas engine shall become the property of the lessee as purchaser thereof for the said sum of £240 so to be paid as aforesaid but until the said several sums shall have been fully paid ... the said Otto gas engine shall remain the sole and absolute property of the owners and lessors.'

Other clauses dealt with care of the engine, marking of it by plates as the property of the owners, and an undertaking by Mr Peel not to remove it from the building in which it was installed without notice to the owners. Specific provisions dealt with failure to make the instalment payments, or the bankruptcy of the lessee: the balance of the full sum of £240 became immediately payable and recoverable by the owners 'who, however, instead of seeking to recover such balance may, if they think fit, seize and resume absolute possession of the said engine wherever the same may be and for this purpose if necessary may break into the premises of the lessee where the said engine may from time to time be or be reasonably thought to be....'

Mr Peel had paid only one instalment, £60, before, on 30 June

1893, he was adjudicated bankrupt.

The issue in the case was the one which is familiar: who owned the gas engine? Crossley Brothers Ltd applied to the court for an order that it should be delivered up to them. The judge refused the order. The Court of Appeal in Ireland ordered the engine to be handed over to the Crossley Brothers. The appellants appealed to the House of Lords.

1.06   Is a retention clause a charge?

In the Court of Appeal counsel for the assignees had argued that the transaction was caught by the 'reputed ownership' or 'apparent ownership' clause of the then current Bankruptcy Act. That Court ruled against them on this point. In the House of Lords, that argument was abandoned. Since a similar clause in the Bankruptcy Act, 1914, may have some relevance where goods are supplied to a private individual or a partnership, as distinct from the situation where the customer is a limited or unlimited liability company, it is discussed in detail subsequently in [6.05].

The thrust of the argument for the appellant assignees in the House of Lords was that the contract was only a colourable device to cloak the true transaction between the parties: that the real relationship between the parties was that of seller and purchaser, with the seller having a charge on the gas engine for the unpaid purchase money. If so, since the charge was not registered under the Bills of Sale Acts, 1878 and 1882, it was void.

These Acts, which are still in force, provide that documents recording mortgages of certain chattels, where the owner remains in possession, must be registered in the central office of the Supreme Court within seven days of their creation (section 8, 1882). If not registered, the security is void. The Acts do not apply to mortgages and charges over chattels which are created by limited liability companies: *re Standard Manufacturing Co. Ltd* (1891). So the only practical application is where the chattels are owned by an individual who creates a mortgage or charge over them. But section 95 of the Companies Act, 1948 requires registration by a company if the document would have to be registered under the Act by any individual.

In recent cases, it has been suggested that a retention of title clause to goods might, in certain circumstances of supply to a company, amount to an outright sale to the buyer and the subsequent immediate mortgage or charge back to the seller. If so, it might require registration under section 95 of the Companies Act, 1948. The exact effect of that section and the only circumstances in which this could arise are discussed later [6.13].

The effect of the Bill of Sales Act, 1882, was described by Lord Herschell L.C.:

'Under the Act, where a bankrupt has transferred the property in his goods to another person, or given that person rights in the nature of rights of property over them, if the goods remain in his possession and he becomes bankrupt, his assignees in bankruptcy can claim the goods ... unless the instrument carrying out the transaction has been registered as a bill of sale.'

His Lordship then continued:

'But, of course, in order to make out that the assignees have a title to this engine under the Bills of Sale Act, it is absolutely essential to prove that the property in the engine, at some time or other, had passed to the bankrupt.

'If the property never passed to the bankrupt, he can never have conveyed it or assigned it, or given the right to seize, or have given any rights over it within the meaning of the Bills of Sale Act....

'Upon an agreement to sell, it depends upon the intention of the parties, whether the property passes or does not pass....

'Here the parties have in terms expressed their intention, and said that the property shall not pass till the full purchase money is paid.

'I know no reason to prevent that being a perfectly lawful agreement.'

Lord Watson supplemented the Lord Chancellor's observation by remarking that:

'It is perfectly plain that the agreement is one of sale and purchase and nothing else.

'It does not in the least follow that, because there is an

agreement of sale and purchase, the property in the thing which is the subject matter of the contract has passed to the purchaser.

'That is a question which entirely depends upon the intention of the parties. The law permits them to settle the point for themselves by any intelligible expression of their intention.'

The other law lords concurred.

The case of *McEntire and Maconchy* v. *Crossley Brothers Ltd* became the foundation upon which the vast expansion of conditional instalment sale agreements, otherwise known as 'deferred sale agreements' or 'suspensive sale agreements' took place, just as the other House of Lords' decision, which follows it immediately in the law reports, *Helby* v. *Matthews and Ors* (1895) became the foundation of hire purchase transactions. In fact, it can be said that upon these two cases hangs all the law and the profits of consumer credit.

But what was not realised at the time was the valuable assistance this decision could give to unpaid sellers.

1.07   The *Romalpa* case

The full possibilities of the conditional sale did not strike most manufacturers and suppliers until the case of *Aluminium Industrie Vaassen B.V.* v. *Romalpa Aluminium Ltd* was heard in the Court of Appeal in 1976. The case was concerned with the supply by a Dutch company of aluminium foil to an English company for resale in the form in which it was delivered.

It will be necessary to analyse this case in depth in due course (see Chapter 7), but it is sufficient at the moment to say that the capriciousness of English litigation is well illustrated by it.

The retention of title clause used was an inelegant translation from the Dutch and, in fact, the contract of sale, including the clause, was expressly made subject to Dutch law. Neither counsel raised the issue of the foreign law, and neither the High Court nor the Court of Appeal received any evidence of the law of sale applicable in the Netherlands.

Had these issues been discussed, the court might have discovered that in Dutch law retention of title clauses deposited with chambers of commerce or district courts are not effective notice to a buyer and it may not recognise a contractual right to assign book debts which do not yet exist or, as English lawyers would put it, the present assignment of future choses in action.

The case was decided on the basis that English law applied.

The Court of Appeal, as Lord Justice Templeman said in the *Borden* case,

'looked with sympathy on an invention designed to provide some protection for one class of unsecured creditors, namely unpaid sellers of goods.'

The Court of Appeal chose not to apply the *contra proferentem* rule, that documents drafted by one party should be construed strictly against that party; they ignored the very real possibility that the clause was void for uncertainty; and they elected to make it a viable contract by implying a power for the buyer to re-sell the goods and held that there was a duty on the part of the buyer to account to the seller for the proceeds; they ignored the inconsistency between such a duty to account for the proceeds of sale to the seller immediately and an express term which granted the buyer seventy-five days credit. It is true, however, to say that none of these points appears to have been argued fully, or indeed at all, before the Court of Appeal.

Other courts subsequently have been less sympathetic to retention of title clauses. It is submitted that, for the reasons given by Lord Justice Templeman, they ought to be, provided the clauses are properly drafted, although as that judge conceded,

'There is no logical reason why this class of creditor should be favoured as against other creditors such as the suppliers of consumables and services.'

Perhaps the answer to that comment is that most suppliers of services, such as solicitors and barristers, already take effective steps to ensure that their services do not go unrewarded. The supplier of goods is rarely able to demand payment in advance.

1.08 English cases since *Romalpa*

Cases subsequent to the *Romalpa* decision have introduced elements of confusion into the law.

Borden (U.K.) Ltd v. *Scottish Timber Products Ltd* (1978) was concerned with the sale of urea-formaldehyde resin for use in the manufacture of chipboard. Chipboard is made from three qualities of desiccated timber: surface dust, 'intermediate' and 'core flakes'. These are mixed with an adhesive made from the urea-formaldehyde resin mixed with wax emulsion and hardeners and the whole is then compressed. The production costs of the final product, chipboard, was said in the course of the evidence to be apportioned: timber 24%, resin 17%.

So that in essence two types of chattel, timber and resin, were being combined, in roughly equal values, to produce the final product.

In *re Bond Worth Ltd* (1979) (see also Chapter 8) Monsanto Ltd sold a synthetic fibre named Acrilan to manufacturers, Bond Worth Ltd, for incorporation into carpets made by them. The Acrilan mixed with reprocessed fibres. This, the process, was subsidiary into two categories: 'white yarn' composed solely of new Acrilan of various types, and 'grey yarn' composed of new Acrilan mixed with reprocessed fibres. This the process was described by the judge: 'Once fibres have been blended into yarn, either white or grey, there is no commercial method of separating them again.' The yarn was then dyed, processed, and woven into carpet with a backing thread, not supplied by Monsanto, which in due course was backed with latex.

The final product therefore was substantially made from Monsanto's Acrilan, processed by Bond Worth, with the addition of some dye materials from other sources and a latex backing. In spite of 800 pages of affidavits, the judge was not supplied with any breakdown of the costs of the final product. Although he did not so conclude, it would appear that in reality the final product was substantially made from Monsanto's Acrilan, after it has been processed, and that the other chattels combined with it were in very minor proportions.

These two cases raised difficult questions in English law as to whether ownership is possible in admixed materials.

To resolve these questions, it will be necessary to look not only at English common law but also at Roman law, the basis of present continental law and the law of the United States.

n.b. Clough Mill v Martin [1984] Times 22 Nov
    FT 20 Nov
w.r.t. unsold goods.
    3 AllER 982
    CA.

1.09 Supply 'on consignment'

The practice has also grown up in the United Kingdom of supplying components 'on consignment'. This practice is not expressly recognised by the Sale of Goods Act 1979, unless it be sale or return subject to rule 4 of section 18.

When in 1980 the lorry manufacturers Fodens passed into receivership, there were on their premises engines, provided on consignment by Rolls Royce, which had not been fitted to lorries, others which had been fitted to lorries on the premises, and others fitted to lorries in dealers' premises. Title was retained until payment.

On counsel's advice, the receiver accepted that all these engines, whether affixed to vehicles or not, remained the property of Rolls Royce.

1.10 Draft directive of the EEC

The EEC has, from time to time, in its efforts to harmonise trading conditions in the common market, produced draft clauses for retention of title which it, some day, intends to require the constituent countries to legislate as part of their domestic law. No attention, in this book, has been paid to these drafts since it is unlikely that they will become law in this century.

1.11 Purpose for which goods are required

The English law of the sale of goods is extraordinarily deficient in two respects.

Firstly, boxes of matches, multi-million pound oil tankers or aircraft are all chattels in law and subject to exactly the same rules governing contracts for their sale. Other systems of law draw a distinction between fungibles, and goods for consumption and other movables.

Secondly, the purpose for which the buyer requires the goods is irrelevant. The same law applied to a pound of apples bought at a greengrocers for consumption as to a shipload of apples bought for resale.

This book ignores retail sales to consumers, since that would involve, amongst other things, investigating the Consumer Credit Act 1974. Hire purchase and conditional sales to consumers are a different topic.

Trade sales may be divided into these categories:

(1) Goods bought for consumption: e.g. fodder to be fed to cattle, or coal to be fired in a furnace.
(2) Goods bought to be resold substantially in the form as they are purchased; e.g. clothes.
(3) Goods bought to be incorporated in another chattel substantially as they are purchased: e.g. components for a motor car.
(4) Goods bought for the purpose of so admixing with other materials and to be processed so as to constitute substantially a new chattel: e.g. resin and fibres, to cite the goods involved in the two leading cases mentioned above.
(5) Goods bought with the intention that they will cease to exist as chattels: e.g. building materials, which on their incorporation into a building or their affixation to land lose their identity as chattels.

To be effective, retention of title clauses must take into consideration the purpose for which goods are bought. There is little purpose in seeking to enforce proprietorship in the ultimate product of cowcake.

Chapter 2

Terms of the Contract?

2.01 A term of the agreement to sell

Before a retention of title clause can have any effect it must be a term of the contract of sale.

In all the leading English cases mentioned so far, there was a dispute as to whether or not the retention clause was included as a term of the contract.

2.02 Incorporation of the term in the *Romalpa* case

The plaintiffs in the *Romalpa* case, Aluminium Industrie Vaassen (A.I.V.), alleged that the clause was a term of the contract with Romalpa Ltd, either expressly or impliedly. The defendants admitted that it did apply to trade that had been carried on previously between A.I.V. and a partnership called Romalpa Aluminium, prior to the plaintiffs beginning to do business with the limited company Romalpa Aluminium Ltd on 1 September 1979, but contended that the clause did not apply to dealings with A.I.V. thereafter.

Mr Justice Mocatta, the trial judge, having considered the facts, concluded that the general selling terms and conditions as applied to the dealings between A.I.V. and the partnership Romalpa Aluminium, also applied to dealings between the plaintiffs and the defendants. There is no published report of his findings on that issue, but in the Court of Appeal, Lord Justice Roskill adverted to the circumstances of the incorporation by reference:

'The plaintiffs did their business on certain general conditions of sale dated February 1971 which were deposited or registered with all district or county courts in Holland.... Those conditions were in Dutch, but there was what one might describe as an authentic and specially prepared, though not very well expressed, English translation of the Dutch conditions. On 4 April 1972, the plaintiffs obtained from the partnership [Romalpa Aluminium], the signature of the two partners on a copy of that English translation. The conditions were expressed to be subject to Dutch law, the Amsterdam court being given exclusive jurisdiction....'

Later, said his lordship, the company took over the business carried on by the partnership and continued to do business on those terms.

'Individual invoices covering specific transactions incorporated both in Dutch and in English what was described as 'an epitome' of the plaintiff's general conditions.... One hesitates to criticise such a document, for one knows the difficulties of translation of this type of document from one language to another; but it cannot be said that the English translation is happy.

'Clause 13 (the retention of title clause) is not referred to in the epitome at all − an omission on which the defendants placed considerable reliance in connection with their submission that, though the general conditions had governed the relationship of the plaintiffs with the partnership, they never governed the plaintiffs' relationship with the defendants, notwithstanding that exactly the same printed form of invoice was used....'

Lord Justice Roskill then adopted the findings of fact made by Mr Justice Mocatta:

'The full deposited terms, including clause 13, did apply to every order placed by the defendants with the plaintiffs. I say that, firstly, because the acknowledged form referred at the front to the epitome behind and clause 13 was in fact part of the general selling terms and conditions filed with the Dutch county courts.... Secondly, if there were any doubts on this point, I would have no hesitation in holding that the full terms including clause 13, were impliedly agreed to apply to each order.'

In the judgment of Lord Justice Megaw, he describes the documents in existence. An Acknowledgement of Order bore on its face the words 'Vide epitome of our General Selling Terms at the back'. The so-called epitome on the back, which included no reference to the retention of title clause 13, purported to describe 'the General Selling Terms and Conditions ... which general selling terms and conditions are filed at the Record Office of all County Courts in the Netherlands'.

It is not proposed in this book to comment on those findings of the trial judge and the Court of Appeal. It is sufficient to say that the company, because of previous transactions by the partnership from which it had acquired the business, and because of the actual admitted knowledge of the directors, was saddled with the vital clause 13 as a term of the conditions of sale.

The courts did not decide that to print on the face of an Acknowledgement of Order a reference to an epitome on the back of terms deposited in Dutch in some local courts in the Netherlands was sufficient notice as to incorporate those terms into the contract. In fact, Lord Justice Megaw said that he did not resile from the observations he had made in *Thornton* v. *Shoe Lane Parking Ltd* (1971)

'Where the particular condition relied upon involves a sort of restriction that is not shown to be usual in that class of contract, a defendant must show that his intention to attach an unusual condition of that particular nature was fairly brought to the notice of the other party.'

Retention of title clauses will not be implied, and had the transactions between A.I.V. and Romalpa Ltd taken place between parties coming afresh to do business with no antecedent transactions between them, it is most unlikely that the vital clause 13 would have been held to be a term of the contract of sale.

The fact that the buyer knows that there are conditions imposed by the seller is not notice of the contents of those conditions: *British Crane Hire* v. *Ipswich Plant Hire* (1975).

2.03   Incorporation of the term in the *Bond Worth* case

The procedure for ordering the Acrilan used for the manufacture of carpets in this case was described by the trial judge:

> 'Bond Worth's orders were submitted in writing on printed order forms.... They were then acknowledged by Monsanto in writing on a series of printed confirmation notes, but on a piece-meal basis, so that each confirmation note would relate to less than the full quantity ordered and, correspondingly, two or more confirmation notes would have to be sent before the full quantity was covered. It appears that each confirmation note was accompanied by a set of Monsanto's standard conditions of sale...
>
> 'Paragraph 10 of the conditions of sale read as follows:

> > "This contract constitutes the full understanding of the parties and a full and exclusive statement of the terms of their agreement. Except as provided in Section 1 hereof, no conditions, understanding or agreement purpotrating [*sic*] to modify or vary the terms of this contract shall be binding unless made in writing and signed by the party to be bound and no modifications shall be effected by the acknowledgement or acceptance of purchase orders or shipment instructions containing terms or conditions at variance or in addition to those set forth...."

> 'The conditions of sale, however, contained no provision expressly reserving to Monsanto any legal or beneficial property or interest in the goods pending payment of the full purchase price.'

His lordship held on the facts that each of the 29 contracts with which he was concerned were not concluded by the acceptance of the order placed by Bond Worth by the issue of a confirmation note by Monsanto, but when the goods in question were actually delivered to and accepted by Bond Worth.

On 30 June 1976, Monsanto wrote a letter addressed to Bond Worth:

'Dear Sirs,

Change in Conditions of Sale
Would you please note that with effect from July 1st, 1976, we are amending our standard terms of contract insofar as all future business will be conducted on normal terms and conditions of sale, except that the following Clause shall be incorporated into any contract to the exclusion of any conflicting provisions in our standard terms as presently appears on our confirmation or orders.

(a)   The risk in the goods passes to the buyer upon delivery, but equitable and beneficial ownership shall remain with us until full payment has been received (each order being considered as a whole), or until prior resale, in which case our beneficial entitlement shall attach to the proceeds of resale or to the claim for such proceeds.

(b)   Should the goods become constituents of or be converted into other products while subject to our equitable and beneficial ownership we shall have the equitable and beneficial ownership in such other products as if they were solely and simply the goods and accordingly sub-clause (a) shall as appropriate apply to such other products.

We would appreciate your acknowledgement that this clause now applies to future deliveries to your goodselves by signing the attached copy letter and returning it to us.'

The company secretary of Bond Worth signed the copy and returned it to Monsanto.

Notwithstanding that letter, Monsanto continued to issue with their confirmation notes, conditions of sale which made no reference to these terms and in fact prohibited any alteration from the terms printed.

Was the retention clause contained in the letter a term of the contract of sale in these circumstances?

His lordship made a finding of fact:

'So long as Bond Worth remained apparently good for the money, the retention of title clause seems for practical purposes to have been forgotten by both the interested parties.'

His conclusion, therefore, was by no means inevitable. He said:

'On the face of it, two points seem to me clear in relation to this correspondence. First, Monsanto thereby proposed and Bond Worth thereby agreed that notwithstanding any conflicting provisions appearing in Monsanto's printed standard conditions of sale (such as condition 10 in particular) the retention of title clause should be deemed to be incorporated in any future contract for the sale and purchase of any goods which might thereafter be delivered by Monsanto to Bond Worth.

'Secondly, both parties must be taken to have intended that the agreement thus concluded should have legal effect.

'In these circumstances my initial reaction to this correspondence is to give effect to the agreement embodied in it, unless there is some compelling reason to the contrary.'

That conclusion does not appear to be supported by the letter itself. That announced a future intention to amend the standard terms of contract: '... with effect from July 1st, 1976, we are amending our standard terms of contract....' No such amendment took place and, on the judge's own finding, the parties forgot all about the letter.

Another judge might well on those facts have concluded that the retention of title terms formed no part of the contract of sale since the offer was made by the issue of a confirmation note to which was attached the unamended conditions of sale, purporting to be as inviolable as the law of the Medes and Persians, and the acceptance was by the act of receiving delivery of goods, and each delivery constituted a separate contract.

2.04   The battle of the forms

These two cases illustrate how narrowly the retention of title clause was held to be part of the contract of sale. Such disputes are likely to be common since what frequently happens is:

Round one: intending buyer asks for quotation on his printed form which contains the terms on which the buyer is willing to do business.

Round two: intending supplier quotes on his own printed terms and conditions of supply, which include a retention of title clause. *Round three:* buyer places an order on his own printed order form which, inter alia, rejects the inclusion of any retention of title clause, usually by stating that the terms set out in the buyer's order form alone shall govern the contract.

Round four: goods are supplied with a delivery note repeating the supplier's terms and conditions, including the retention of title clause. The buyer's gateman signs for the goods and takes them into stock.

The question is, is there a contract for the sale of goods and, if so, on what terms?

On basic principles, the answer may be that there is no contract of any kind. Traditionally, unless the parties are agreed as to all essential terms, there is no contract. That, at least, is what students are taught, in accordance with the cases of *Hyde* v. *Wrench* (1840); *Neale* v. *Merrett* (1930); *Northland Airlines Ltd* v. *Dennis Ferranti Ltd* (1970), etc.

The learned editor of *Cheshire and Fifoot on the Law of Contract* (9th edition, page 151) appears to support this view, while conceding that in practice the courts will not adopt it but try to give some commercial effect to what the parties have done. The learned editor of *Anson on Contract* (24th edition, page 37), however, supports the view that there should be held to be a binding contract in spite of the old rules.

It should also be borne in mind that if goods are in fact supplied, but on the facts there is no express contract, the courts may imply a quasi-contractual obligation on the buyer to pay for goods received on the basis of a *quantum valebant* (i.e. the market value of the goods which may not be the agreed price) and in that case the transaction will not incorporate any term about retention of title. (See also S. 8 (2) of the Sale of Goods Act 1979.)

Excluding 'no express contract' and 'no implied contract', as answers to the problem, if there is a contract is it on:

(a) the seller's terms, or
(b) the buyer's terms?

In general the courts in England have inclined to the view that the winner of the battle of the forms is 'the last past the post'. In other words, if goods are accepted by the buyers on certain conditions put forward by the seller, those conditions apply.

Those were the findings of the court in *British Road Services Ltd* v. *Arthur V. Crutchley & Co. Ltd* (1968), where however, there had been previous dealings between the parties. A load of whisky was delivered by British Road Services to a warehouse belonging to the defendants who stamped the plaintiff's delivery note 'Received on A.V.C.'s Conditions'. The whisky was stolen while in the defendants' possession. On whose conditions were the goods stored: on those contained in the plaintiffs' printed delivery note or on the defendants' condition annexed by the rubber stamped words? Needless to say, the conditions were entirely incompatible. The Court of Appeal held that the defendant's conditions were incorporated in their contract with the plaintiffs by reason of the rubber stamp. But had the lorry driver power or authority to bind his employers?

In the later case of *Butler Machine Tool Co. Ltd* v. *Ex-Cell-O Corporation (England) Ltd* (1979), the court again opted for the 'last past the post' solution.

Round one: the plaintiffs offered a machine tool to the defendants on terms containing a price fluctuation clause.

Round two: the defendants accepted the offer on their own standard order form, which had no price fluctuation clause, but which had a tear off section which read: 'We accept your order on the Terms and Conditions stated thereon'.

Round three: the plaintiffs completed and returned this slip to the defendants.

Round four: the plaintiffs supplied the machine tool without imposing other terms on their delivery note.

Later, the plaintiffs sought to claim an escalation in price under their price fluctuation clause. The Court of Appeal held that the goods had been brought on the buyers' (the defendants') terms and those terms contained no provisions for escalation.

2.05   The battle of the forms in the USA

In the United States a not entirely satisfactory attempt has been made to resolve the problem by article 2 - 207 of the Uniform Commercial Code:

'(1) A definite and reasonable expression of acceptance or a written confirmation which is sent within a reasonable time operates as an acceptance even though it states terms additional to or different from those offered or agreed upon...

(2) The additional terms are to be construed as proposals for addition to the contract. Between merchants such terms become part of the contract unless:

   (a) the offer expressly limits acceptance to the terms of the offer;
   (b) they materially alter it; or
   (c) notification or objection to them has already been given or is given within a reasonable time after notice of them is received.

(3) Conduct by both parties which recognises the existence of a contract is sufficient to establish a contract for sale although the writings of the parties do not otherwise establish a contract. In such a case the terms of the particular contract consist of those terms on which the writings of the parties agree, together with any supplementary terms incorporated under other provisions of this Act.'

It is therefore essential for a seller who wishes to include a retention of title clause to ensure that his terms prevail in the contract of sale. To include the terms only on an invoice may well be too late. By that time an agreement for the sale of goods may well have been concluded — without the term.

Chapter 3

Types of Retention of Title Clauses

3.01   Simple retention of title clauses

The first class of retention of title clause is the simple one. Two examples have already been quoted in [1.03]. Other found in practice include:

'The ownership of any goods delivered shall remain with us until the full invoice price has been paid.'

'The property in the goods shall not pass to you until payment in full of the price to us.'

'The property in all goods shall remain with us until payment in full has been received.'

'The title in the goods does not pass to our customer until they have been paid for in full.'

'Notwithstanding that the buyer or his agent obtain possession of the goods, the ownership therein shall remain in the Company [the seller] until such time as payment is made in full to the Company.'

'Notwithstanding delivery the property in the goods shall remain in the Company until the customer has paid in full therefor.'

'Title of goods supplied shall not pass to the customer until payment has been made of the full contract price.'

'The risk in the goods passes to the buyer upon delivery but ownership shall remain in us until full payment has been received.'

'The property in the goods shall pass to the Stockist only when the goods which have been delivered to the Stockist have been paid in full.'

Problems that may arise with simple clauses are:

(1) They do not deal with the question of risk of damage or destruction of the goods. Under English law the passing of ownership and risk normally go together. Section 20 of the Sale of Goods Act 1979, states:

'(1) Unless otherwise agreed, the goods remain at the seller's risk until the property in them is transferred to the buyer, but when the property in them is transferred to the buyer the goods are at the buyer's risk whether delivery has been made or not.'

If title is retained until payment, it is prudent therefore for the seller to provide that the risk shall pass to the buyer on delivery. In only one of the clauses quoted above was this precaution taken, with the result that all the other clauses quoted are deficient in that the sellers would have lost their title to the goods, and all right to payment, if the goods perished by fire, theft or any other way in the absence of an express agreement or acknowledgement by the buyer that the risk should be borne by him. A seller with a retention clause should therefore either provide by the terms of his contract that the risk passes to the intending buyer on delivery, or himself insure the goods.

(2) These conditions do not give a right, nor does the general law, for the seller to enter on the buyer's premises to repossess the goods. Only an express term of the contract of sale can do this.
    Often, clauses provide for this:

'Notwithstanding that the Buyer or his agents obtain possession of the goods the ownership therein will remain in the Company [the seller] until such time as payment is made in full to the Company, which shall be entitled to all rights of access to the Buyer's premises to enforce its rights hereunder.'

'If payment is overdue in whole or in part the Company [the seller] may (without prejudice to any of its other rights) recover or recall the goods or any of them and may enter upon the customer's premises for that purpose. These Conditions constitute authority for any third party authorised by the Company to enter upon any other premises wheresoever the goods are situate for the purpose of recovering the goods or any of them.'

'If payment of the total price or other sums is not made on the due date' [thirty days after despatch of products] 'the supplier shall have the right with or without prior notice at any time to retake possession of the whole or any part of the products (and for that purpose to go upon any premises occupied by the purchaser thereof) without prejudice to any other remedy of the supplier.'

'The Company shall be entitled and the Stockist hereby grants to the Company a licence to enter upon the premises of the Stockist during normal business hours for the purpose of removing such goods and to remove such goods from the Stockist's premises.'

'The Company shall be entitled to enter upon any premises of the customer for the purpose of removing such goods and new products manufactured with such goods from the premises, with a view to clear any outstanding debt.'

'On termination of the customer's power of sale in accordance with the foregoing conditions, the customer must place the goods and new products manufactured with them at the disposal of the Company which reserves the right to enter upon any premises for the purpose of removing such goods and new products, such rights to include severance where necessary from realty.'

(3) Such clauses may in the case of a buyer who is not a corporate body be defeated by the 'reputed' ownership provision of the Bankruptcy Act, 1914; see [6.05].

(4)   Such clauses may, in the case of a buyer who is in possession of the goods and resells them to a sub-purchaser who knows nothing of the retention clause, be defeated by the provisions of section 25 (1) of the Sale of Goods Act 1979 [4.11].

3.02   The 'current account' clause

A more sophisticated form of the retention of title clause is one where the property is not to pass until all other goods sold by the seller to the buyer have been paid for in full. In France this clause is known as a *compte courant* clause, and in Germany as a *Konto-korrent* clause.

At one time in Germany doubt was expressed about the validity of such clauses, since it was contended that ownership of goods subject to such a clause might never pass to the buyer and it was therefore inconsistent with it being a contract of sale. These doubts were however resolved by a decision of the German Supreme Court as long ago as 1935.

A typical example is to be found in the *Romalpa* clause itself:

'The ownership of the material to be delivered by A.I.V. will only be transferred to purchaser when he has met all that is owing to A.I.V., no matter on what grounds. Until the date of payment, purchaser, if A.I.V. so desires, is required to store his materials in such a way that it is clearly the property of A.I.V.'

Other examples seen in the United Kingdom are as follows:

'The property in the products shall remain in the supplier until the payment of the total price thereof and any other payments due to the supplier from the purchaser have been made.'

'Ownership in the goods shall remain with the Company until such time as the purchaser has paid in full all that he owes to the Company.'

'Until full payment has been received by the Company for all goods supplied at any time by the Company (1) the property in the goods shall remain in the Company....'

'Until such time as full payment has been received by the Company for all goods whatsoever supplied all goods shall remain the property of the Company.'

'Notwithstanding delivery of the goods or any part thereof the property in the goods shall remain in the seller until the purchaser has paid the purchase price in full as well as any other payments due to the seller whether hereunder or in respect of any other liability to the Seller whatsoever.'

3.03   The continuing retention clause

These clauses purport to extend the retention of title clause from the buyer to any purchaser from him and provide that any such purchasers shall not get title until the purchase price has been paid. In France such a provision is known as a *réservation prolongée*, and in Germany as a *weitergeleitet Eigentumsvorbehalt*.

A clause which attempts to do this is:

'Title of goods supplied shall not pass to the customer or to any person claiming under him until payment has been made of the full contract price. In case of non-payment the Company shall be entitled to repossess or trace the goods or the proceeds of sale from the customer or its liquidator or receiver or from any purchaser or other person drawing title from the customer.'

This type of clause is not frequently found in England because there are two serious problems with it:

(1)   The English doctrine of privity of contract prevents a person who is not a party to the contract having obligations imposed upon him by it. Since sub-purchasers are not parties to the original contract of sale they are not bound by such terms, even if they know of them: *McGruther* v. *Pitcher* (1904); *Port Line Ltd* v. *Ben Steamers* (1958). There are, however, numerous exceptions to this, including terms which 'run with the land'. It has been suggested that if the goods are identifiable, the same principle may apply.

(2)   Section 25 (1) of the Sale of Goods Act 1979 (previously section 25 (2) of the Sale of Goods Act, 1893) provides:

'Where a person having bought or agreed to buy goods obtains with the consent of the seller, possession of the goods ... delivery on transfer by that person ... of the goods ... under any sale ... to any person receiving the same in good faith and without notice of any lien or other right of the original seller of the goods, has the same effect as if the person making the delivery ... were a mercantile agent in possession of the goods ... with the consent of the owner.'

In other words, a sub-purchaser who knows nothing of the retention of title clause will get a good title. Section 25 (1) overrides the retention of title clause. See [4.12].

In other jurisdictions, obligations are imposed on a buyer to include a retention of title clause in favour of the seller in any contracts he makes and to take on an undertaking from sub-purchasers from him that they will impose the same condition on persons to whom they may resell. The same is possible in English law.

3.04   The 'proceeds of sale' clause

This clause authorises the buyer to resell the goods but provides that the proceeds of sale shall be held by him as an agent or trustee for the seller until the price owed by the buyer has been paid. In France such a provision is known as a *réservation étendue,* and in Germany as a *verlängerte Eigentumsvorbehalt.* It is supplemented frequently by the provision that the buyer's rights against his sub-purchaser shall be held in trust for the seller and/or shall be assigned by the buyer to the seller on demand.

Such clauses are frequently found in England:

'The title in the goods does not pass to our customer until they have been paid for in full and if our customer sells the goods before the goods have been paid for, then we have the right to the proceeds of such sale.'

'In the event of the Buyer reselling or otherwise disposing of the goods or any part thereof before the property therein has passed to him [under the basic retention of title clause] then the Buyer will, until payment in full to the Company [the seller] of the price of the goods, hold in trust for the Company all his rights under any such contract of re-sale or any other contract in pursuance of which the goods or any part thereof are disposed of, or any contract by which property comprising the said goods or any part thereof is or is to be disposed of, and any monies or other consideration received by him thereunder.'

* should be express — see *Re Andrabell* [1984] 3 All ER 407

'Notwithstanding delivery the property in the goods shall remain in the Company [the seller] until the customer has paid in full therefore, and the customer hereby declares itself trustee of the goods for the Company until such payment is made and the customer shall hold the goods and any proceeds of sale of the goods and any rights arising from any sale thereof as trustee for the Company.'

'Ownership in the goods shall remain with the Company [the seller] until such time as the purchaser has paid in full all that he owes to the Company. Until that time the purchaser shall keep the goods for the Company in his capacity as fiduciary owner, although the purchaser shall be entitled to sell the goods to a third party within the normal carrying on of his business on the conditions that such sale shall be for the Company's account and, if the Company so require, the purchaser shall hand over to the Company any claims emanating from the sub-sale that he has against his buyer.'

'The risk in the goods passes to the buyer upon delivery, but equitable and beneficial ownership shall remain with us until full payment has been received (each order being considered as a whole), or until prior re-sale in which case our beneficial entitlement shall attach to the proceeds of re-sale on to the claim for such proceeds.'

'In the event of the buyer re-selling or otherwise disposing of the goods or any part thereof before the property has passèd to him, the buyer will, until payment is made in full to the Company [the seller] of the price of the goods, hold in trust for the Company all his rights under any such contract of sale or other contract in pursuance of which the goods or any part thereof are disposed of, or any contract by which property comprising the said goods or any part thereof is or is to be disposed of, and any monies or other consideration received by him thereunder.'

'The Buyer shall be entitled to sell both the goods supplied by the Seller in their original state or manufactured goods incorporating the goods supplied to third parties in the normal course of its business and to deliver them to third parties subject to the condition that the Buyer so long as it has not fully discharged its indebtedness to the Seller shall pass to the Seller the claims the Buyer has against the third parties or the proceeds of sale of goods to third parties.'

'Subject to the following appropriate clauses, the customer shall have the right to sell the goods and new products referred to above in the ordinary course of business on the understanding that the proceeds of any such sale shall belong to the company to whom the customer shall account on demand.'

This clause raises very many problems, as will be seen in subsequent chapters. They include questions such as:

(1) Whether there can be created contractually an assignment of a future choses in action (i.e. the debt owed by the sub-purchaser to the buyer for the re-sale price of the goods).

(2) Whether these terms, in the case of a buyer who is not a corporate body, constitute a 'bill of sale' which has to be registered under the Bills of Sale Acts, 1878 and 1882.

(3) Whether these terms in case of a buyer which is a company incorporated under the Companies Acts constitute a charge which has to be recorded by the company under section 104 of the Companies Act, 1948, and registered at the Companies Registry under section 95 of the same Act.

(4) Whether any of these terms create a valid trust in favour of the seller, or at least a fiduciary obligation.

The short answer to all these questions can be given in an adaptation of the words of Lord Herschell already quoted [1.06]. To show that either (2) or (3) applies 'it is absolutely essential to prove that property in [the goods], at some time or other, had passed to the [buyer]'.

3.05   The aggregation clause

This clause permits the buyer to use the goods to fabricate other products from them or to incorporate the goods into composite products, and purports to vest the ownership of the resulting composite products in the seller to the exclusion of all other suppliers, or as an owner of the products in common with the buyer and all other suppliers who have reserved similar rights in proportion to the value of the goods supplied by them respectively. Such a provision is known in France as a *réservation agrégée,* and in Germany as *erweitete Eigentumsvorbehalt.*

English examples of this type of clause include the following:

'If any of the goods are processed into other goods before payment in full for the goods has been received by the Company [the seller], the goods including all of any other goods as aforesaid shall be the property of the Company, and the customer hereby declares itself trustee of such goods for the Company until such payment is made, and the customer shall hold such goods and any proceeds of sale of such goods and any rights arising from any sale thereof as trustee for the Company.'

'Should the goods become constituents of or be converted into other products while subject to our equitable and beneficial ownership, we shall have the equitable and beneficial ownership in such other products as if they were solely and simply the goods.'

'The Seller and the Buyer agrees that when the goods are manufactured into new objects or are mixed with other goods, or if the goods in any way whatsoever become a constituent of other goods, the Seller shall have the ownership of the new manufactured goods as security for the amount owing to the Seller. The transfer of ownership of the new goods will be considered to have taken place at the moment when the goods supplied by the Seller are converted into the new goods or are mixed with or become a constituent of other goods. Until payment in full is made to the Seller the Buyer shall keep the goods in question for the Seller in its capacity of fiduciary owner and shall store the goods in such a way that they can be recognised as such should the Seller so require.'

'The property in the goods shall remain with the Company [the Seller] in accordance with this Condition and the Company shall be entitled to re-delivery of the goods notwithstanding the subjection of the goods to any admixture or treatment whether by the Stockist or others.'

'Upon determination of the customer's power of sale, the customer shall pass the goods and any new products into which they have been incorporated to the Company [the Seller] in an effort to clear the debt.'

'In cases where the goods or part thereof have been converted into other products, whether or not this involves the addition of any other ingredient or item whatsoever irrespective of the proportions thereof, the conversion shall be deemed to have been made on the

Company's [the Seller's] behalf and legal and beneficial ownership of the resulting products shall pass in full to the Company.'

The problems of clauses of this nature in English law are legion, and will be discussed after consideration of the leading cases.

The chronology of the cases decided by the courts of this country on the various kinds of retention clauses is of importance, and they will therefore be dealt with in strict historical sequence in following chapters.

Chapter 4

Transferring Ownership of Goods

4.01 Title passed only by owner

The fundamental assumption of English law is that nobody who is not himself the owner of goods can make any person who 'buys' from him the owner. This is expressed in the legal maxim *'nemo dat quod non habet'* i.e. 'a man cannot give what he has not got' — a principle women discovered long before the law did.

This is quite different from Roman law and from most European laws which derive from it. But English law provides many exceptions to the principle. These are relevant where a buyer comes into possession of goods subject to a retention of title clause under which the seller remains the owner and then the buyer re-sells the goods to a sub-purchaser with or without the original seller's consent.

The common law rules as to whether and, if so, when, the ownership of goods passed to the buyer under a contract of sale were, with some modification, incorporated in the Sale of Goods Act, 1893. These rules remain substantially unaltered in the present Sale of Goods Act 1979.

4.02 Exception to the general rule

The main exceptions to the rule that only the owner of goods can transfer a title to a buyer are:

agency; estoppel (section 21); sales in Market Overt (section 22);

seller in possession after sale (section 24); buyer in possession after agreement to sell (section 25(1)); mercantile agents or factors under the Factors Act, 1889; goods taken in distress or in execution; innkeepers under the Innkeepers Act, 1878; repairers under the Disposal of Uncollected Goods Act, 1952; sales of motor vehicles under the Hire Purchase Act 1964; and the Unsolicited Goods and Services Act 1971.

The exceptions relevant to the present study are dealt with subsequently.

4.03   Specific or unascertained goods?

At common law, the presumption was, in the absence of agreement to the contrary, that the ownership of the goods passed to the buyer when the contract of sale was made, if the goods were specific or identified at that time; in any other cases, ownership passed when the goods were subsequently delivered to the buyer.

Whether the purchase price had been paid, or whether the seller had agreed to allow the buyer credit was irrelevant. Ownership was retained by the seller if payment had not been made only in these cases where the contract of sale expressly so provided.

The Sales of Goods Act, 1893, modified those rules.

The time at which ownership passes to the buyer still depends upon whether the goods are specific or unascertained.

Specific goods are defined by section 61 of the 1979 Act:

'"Goods" includes all personal chattels other than things in action and money ... and in particular ... includes emblements, industrial growing crops, and things attached to or forming part of the land which are agreed to be severed before sale or under the contract of sale.'

It is material to note that the words 'personal chattels' as defined in the Bills of Sale Act, 1878 include a different definition of 'goods'. Some things therefore are 'goods' for the purpose of the Sale of Goods Act, but not 'goods' for the purposes of the Bills of Sale Act.

It will be noted that neither are exhaustive definitions.

'"Specific goods" means goods identified and agreed upon at the time a contract of sale is made.'

The distinction is between specific or ascertained goods and unascertained goods which may be future goods. In the first the seller only performs his obligations under the contract by delivering the very goods which are the subject matter of the contract. With contracts for unascertained goods, the seller performs his obligations by delivering goods which correspond to the description in the contract.

The Sale of Goods Act 1979 provides that the ownership of unascertained goods cannot pass to the buyer until they are ascertained (section 16). The title to specific goods, on the other hand, can pass immediately after the contract is made if the parties so agree (section 18). Section 16 is a matter of law and is not subject to contrary agreement by the parties.

4.04 The passing of property in unascertained goods
The term 'unascertained goods' may carry one of three possible meanings: namely that the goods have yet to be manufactured or grown by the seller; or, that the goods are purely generic goods (e.g. 100 tons of high tensile steel); or, that the goods are an unidentified portion of a specified whole (e.g. 50 tons out of 100 tons of oil stored at a certain place).

Although the Act does not distinguish between these three kinds of unascertained goods, the rules as to the passing of property and risk necessarily differ in the three cases.

Section 16 lays down the principle that where there is a contract for the sale of unascertained goods, the ownership of the goods cannot pass to the buyer unless and until the goods are ascertained. Section 18, rule 5, then provides that unless a contrary intention is shown, where there is a contract for the sale of unascertained or future goods by description, and goods of that description in a deliverable state are appropriated unconditionally to the contract, either by the buyer or the seller, with the assent of the other of them, the ownership of the goods passes to the buyer. In *D.F. Mount Ltd* v. *Jay and Jay Provisions Ltd*)1960) goods were appropriated under the contract by the seller and the buyer. In *D.F. Mount Ltd* v. *Jay and Jay Provisions Ltd* (1960) re-selling the goods.

Ownership cannot pass until the goods are in a deliverable state. Thus if the seller delivers the goods intended for the buyer to a carrier still mixed with other goods (and therefore still unascertained), ownership cannot pass to the buyer.

Furthermore, ownership cannot pass until identifiable goods have been appropriated under the contract. Thus, in *Healy* v. *Howlett & Sons* (1917) it was held that the ownership of a quantity of mackerel had not passed to the buyer because although the seller had given the railway company, which was to transport a consignment of mackerel, instructions to earmark twenty boxes of mackerel for the buyer, that number of boxes had not been separated from the consignment and so had not been appropriated to the contract.

Moreover, where unascertained goods can only be appropriated to a contract after they have been weighed, measured or tested in order to ascertain the price, the ownership of the goods does not pass to the buyer until this has been done.

In *National Coal Board* v. *Gamble* (1959) coal had been appropriated by the NCB to the contract to supply the defendant with a certain quantity by being loaded on to the buyer's lorry, but it was held that the appropriation was not unconditional until the coal was weighed so as to ascertain the total price payable, and the weight-ticket had been accepted by the buyer.

For the ownership of unascertained goods to pass to the buyer, not only must the goods be identified and appropriated to the contract by the seller or buyer but also the other party must assent to the appropriation.

Usually, it is the seller who makes the appropriation by setting aside or despatching particular goods out of a larger stock in fulfilment of his contractual obligations, and the buyer's assent to the appropriation is shown by his taking delivery of the goods, whether he accepts them as conforming to the contract or not.

The courts have been reluctant to hold that anything less than taking delivery amounts to an assent on the part of the buyer, in the absence of any other express signification of his assent. Thus in *Carlos Federspiel & Co. SA* v. *Charles Twigg & Co. Ltd* (1957) it was held that under an 'f.o.b.' contract the buyer had not assented to an appropriation by the seller of the correct number of goods out of the seller's stock by the seller packing them and marking the packages with the buyer's name and arranging for the carriage of the goods to the buyer by sea and notifying the buyer that all these things had been done, when the buyer had not affirmatively indicated his assent but had merely not notified the seller of any objection.

It is therefore clear that the buyer does not impliedly assent to an appropriation by receiving a notice of appropriation from the seller, however detailed it may be, nor by a carrier taking possession of the goods in order to deliver them to the buyer, unless the carrier is expressly appointed by the buyer to be his agent to give his assent (which is unusual).

On the other hand, express terms of the contract may make the seller the buyer's agent to assent to the appropriation which he makes as seller, and this will be so if the contract expressly provides that when he has appropriated particular goods to the contract, the seller shall hold them as agent or bailee for the buyer.

4.05 Part of bulk goods

The rule, though easy to state, may become difficult to apply when there is a question of ownership of part of a bulk.

The passing of property in an entire bulk, a cargo of grain or a tanker of oil, is a matter for agreement between the parties. They can agree that property shall pass either before the buyer takes delivery, on delivery, or at some subsequent date, including the date when payment is made to the seller.

But English law insists that property cannot pass in part of the bulk until that part is separated from the bulk or is otherwise ascertained or identified, as the result of section 16 of the Sale of Goods Act 1979 which reads:

'Where there is a contract for the sale of unascertained goods, no property in the goods is transferred to the buyer unless and until the goods are ascertained.'

In other words, in English law a buyer cannot buy goods until he knows what goods he is buying.

In *re London Wine* (1975) Mr Justice Oliver held that the sale of a specified number of bottles of wine of a particular claret from a wine cellar conferred no title to the goods on the buyer. In that he followed the Court of Appeal in *re Wait* (1927) where Wait bought 1000 tons of Western White wheat ex *SS Challenger,* which was expected to be loaded in December 1925 in Oregon. The wheat was duly loaded in bulk and an invoice for the 1000 tons forwarded to Wait. He subsequently became bankrupt and the court held that he had acquired no property in the wheat since it had never been severed from the bulk or specifically identified.

Much the same happened in *Hayman* v. *McLintock* (1907). A Glasgow flour merchant imported a cargo of flour from the USA and had it in his warehouse when he became bankrupt. One creditor paid for 424 bags of flour and had been given a delivery note which he had presented to the warehouseman, who accepted it prior to the bankruptcy. But the creditor acquired no title to the goods. Said the judge:

> 'These flour bags were not separately marked and although doubtless, if the buyer had gone to the storekeeper and had got him to put aside the sacks or mark them or put them in another room, that would have passed the property....'

4.06   The United States' rule

There is no such rule in the United States, and the manner in which the Uniform Sales Act and the Uniform Commercial Code deal with sales of part bulk there illustrates that ownership in common is by no means inconsistent with the common law.

Section 17 of the Uniform Sales Act provided that no property in goods that were unascertained should pass by the contract of sale, but it further provided that 'property in an undivided share of ascertained goods may be transferred as provided by section 6.'

Section 6 of the Uniform Sales Act then provided:

'(1) There may be a contract to sell or a sale of an undivided share of goods. If the parties intend to effect a present sale, the buyer, by force of the agreement, becomes owner in common with the owner or owners of the remaining shares.

(2) In the case of fungible goods, there may be a sale of an undivided share of specific mass ... though the number, weight or measure of the goods in the mass, is undivided.'

The Uniform Commercial Code, now in force in most states, provides, in paragraph 2–105 (4):

'An individual share of fungible goods is sufficiently identified to be sold although the quantity of the bulk is not determined. Any agreed portion of such a bulk of any quantity thereof agreed upon by number, weight or other measure may to the extent of the seller's interest in the bulk be sold to the buyer who then becomes an owner in common.'

4.07 Ownership when intended

In English law therefore, the principle is that the goods must be specific or ascertained before property in them can pass to a buyer.

The Sale of Goods Act 1979 provides, as did the 1893 Act, that the ownership of goods sold or contracted to be sold passes to the buyer when the parties intend (section 17). If the contract is not explicit on this matter, it must be determined, having regard to the terms of the contract, the conduct of the parties and the circumstances of the transaction.

Certain presumptions as to the intentions of the parties are set out in the Act in section 18, but the fact that the price remains unpaid, or that the seller has agreed to give credit, does not affect these presumptions.

These presumptions in section 18 are dependent on there being no indication in the parties' agreement or other circumstances of the transaction which make 'a different intention' appear. These days, the courts readily incline to finding a different intention and are reluctant to hold that the property to goods passes to a buyer who has yet to pay for them or take delivery. In *R. V. Ward Ltd* v. *Bignall* (1967), the defendant agreed to buy two cars for £850 and having left £25 in cash went to his bank to get the balance. On the way, he changed his mind. In the course of judgment, the presumption in section 18, rule 1, to the effect that property passes to the buyer when the contract was made, was discussed. Lord Justice Sellers expressed the opinion that the property had not passed to the buyer. This fact that the buyer had:

'agreed to buy the two vehicles ... and paid £25 in cash at the time goes but a little way to establishing that the parties intended the vehicles then and there to become the buyer's property. There was not even a payment by cheque. The buyer went to his bank to get cash and that was to be handed over .... He had not even seen the log books or inquired of their existence. No mention was made of the removal of the vehicles or their insurance....'

Lord Justice Diplock having said that section 17 was the governing rule went on:

> 'In modern times very little is needed to give rise to the inference that the property in specific goods is to pass only on delivery or payment.'

The presumptions as to passing of title contained in section 18 are, of course, irrelevant where there is an express clause reserving title until payment.

4.08   Goods on sale or return

However, rule 4 of section 18 of the Sale of Goods Act 1979 is relevant for it deals with a different situation, where there is no sale or agreement to sell but the goods have passed into the possession of the other party on approval, or on sale or return or, as it is sometimes called, 'on consignment'.

'When goods are delivered to the buyer on approval or on "sale or return" or other similar terms the property in the goods passes to the buyer: —
(a)   when he signifies his approval or acceptance to the seller or does any other act adopting the transaction;
(b)   if he does not signify his approval or acceptance to the seller but retains the goods without giving notice of rejection, then, if a time has been fixed for the return of the goods, on the expiration of that time, and if, no time has been fixed, on the expiration of a reasonable time.'

It must be stressed, again, that this presumption applies only 'unless a different intention appears', so that it is open to the parties to make quite different provisions in their contracts for the passing of title, e.g. for property not to pass before payment.

Although the section appears to be wide enough to cover the situation where goods are supplied unsolicited, in spite of the inept use of the word 'buyer', the better view is that it has no application unless the recipient has requested the goods.

4.09   Involuntary bailees

The question may be relevant where the recipient sells the goods to a third party. Can that third party get a good title under section 25 (1) from an involuntary recipient, even if that recipient has in all honesty decided to purchase the goods? It would appear not.

A similar question arises where the recipient has requested or expressly accepted the goods on approval: *Bradley & Cohn Ltd* v. *Ramsay & Co.* (1912). How can he become 'a buyer in possession' until he has agreed to buy the goods?

It would appear that both an involuntary recipient and the one who requested the goods but has not yet exercised the option to purchase are both bailees of the goods for the owner. The obligations of the bailee in modern times are independent of contract or consent and extend both to involuntary bailees, as where a man by mistake takes the wrong suitcase from the luggage rack of a train, and to sub-bailees. If a bailee sells the goods, he is liable to account to the owner for the proceeds, since a bailee of any kind is in a fiduciary position. The old law, which drew a distinction between bailees for reward and bailees at will, is now largely obsolete except in so far as there may be different duties of care: *Houghland* v. *R. R. Low (Luxury Coaches) Ltd* (1962).

However, it is highly desirable that where goods are supplied under retention conditions, the terms should be spelt out with exactitude in order to avoid litigation. This might indeed decide some interesting issues which, after nearly a century, have yet to be settled, but it will do little to benefit a supplier. In particular the words 'any other act adopting the transaction' have greatly enriched lawyers: *London Jewellers* v. *Attenborough* (1934); *Genn* v. *Winkel* (1912); *Poole* v. *Smith's Car Sales (Balham) Ltd* (1962).

4.10 Title obtained by sub-purchasers

Section 21 (1) and subsequent sections of the Sale of Goods Act 1979 create a number of exceptions to the general rule that a person who has no title to goods cannot confer on a third party a valid title to them. It is not proposed to deal with all the exceptions mentioned in [4.02] but only with the particular case of dispositions made which will be affected by a retention clause.

The question, so far as the seller with a retention of title clause is concerned, is whether the goods remain the original seller's property, if the buyer sells-on those goods to a sub-purchaser; or whether the sub-sale vests the title in the sub-purchaser.

If, according to the basic rule of English law, no title can be passed by anybody who has no title, the original seller can recover his goods from the sub-purchaser irrespective of whether he has paid for them or not. If, however, the sub-purchaser acquires a title, the original seller has no rights against him. If the purchase price paid by the sub-purchaser has been paid to the buyer who is selling-on, the original owner has to fall back on his equitable trading rights. If the purchase price has not been paid to the buyer selling-on by the time a receiver or liquidator has been appointed, the proceeds, if the retention clause has been properly drafted, will be the original seller's.

It is therefore of great importance to see how a sub-purchaser can acquire title to the goods under the Sale of Goods Act even though *his* seller has none to pass to him because title is retained by the *original* seller.

4.11   Title by estoppel

Section 21 of the Sale of Goods Act 1979 deals with one circumstance in which a title to goods may be acquired by a buyer from a person who is not the owner and has no title to them. This, like the other cases which will follow, is an instance where the buyer *obtains* a good title rather than that a title *passes* to him. It reads:

Section 21 (1): 'Subject to this Act, where goods are sold by a person who is not their owner and who does not sell them under the authority or with the consent of the owner the buyer acquires no better title to the goods than the seller had, *unless the owner of the goods is by his conduct precluded from denying the seller's authority to sell.*'

There are two aspects to this. An agent with limited authority may appear to a buyer to have unlimited authority. For example, if the owner of goods entrusts them to somebody else to sell for him but not under £1000 and that person sells them at a lower price, the buyer will normally get a good title. An agent is only an agent if he has the actual authority of his principal; but he may also have what is called 'ostensible authority'. The principal is bound by his agent's ostensible authority on the principle set out in the italicised words of section 21 quoted above.

To lawyers this is known as 'estoppel'. If the owner of goods holds somebody out as the agent to dispose of them, he is 'estopped' from denying that person's authority to sell them.

The other aspect is to be seen where the true owner allows some other person to appear to the world as if he were the owner. An illustration is to be found in *Stoneleigh Finance* v. *Phillips* (1965) where the owner of a car who wished to raise money on it by way of a hire purchase transaction signed a document for a finance company which stated that a car dealer had the sole, unencumbered ownership of the car. The true owner was estopped from denying that the car dealer was the owner.

The words of section 21 are regrettably vague and do little to help resolve the problem of whether a seller who passes goods to a buyer with a retention of title clause, who knows that the buyer is going to re-sell the goods as his own, is estopped from denying that a sub-purchaser has become the owner. In *Commonwealth Trust* v. *Akotey* (1926), a decision of the Judicial Committee of the Privy Council (and not therefore strictly binding on the English courts), it was said that to 'permit goods to go into the possession of another, with all the insignia of possession thereof and of apparent title, and to leave it open to go behind that possession ... and upset a purchase of the goods made for full value and in good faith, would bring confusion into mercantile transactions'. However, that case has been much criticised, and was not followed in *Mercantile Bank of India Ltd* v. *Central Bank of India Ltd* (1938).

The position appears to be that to allow a buyer to have possession of the goods, even if it is known by the seller who retains title that the buyer will process and re-sell them as his own, is not sufficient to estop the seller. But possession plus any *indicium* (or proof) of title will estop the owner. But it was held in *Central Newbury Car Auctions* v. *Unity Finance* (1957) that a motor car log book was neither a 'document of title' under section 1 (4) of the Factors Act, 1889, nor an *indicium* of title.

Of course if the seller has consented to the buyer reselling the goods as owner thereof, he will be estopped from denying the fact.

4.12 Title from buyer in possession

Section 25 (1) of the Sale of Goods Act, 1979 (originally section 9 of the Factors Act, 1889, and section 25 (2) of the Sale of

Goods Act, 1893) deals with the position where a person who has bought, or agreed to buy, certain goods obtains the possession of the goods, or the documents of title to them, with the consent of the seller and sells, pledges or disposes of those goods or documents of title to a person who receives them in good faith and without notice of any lien or other right of the original seller. (A lien is the right of somebody who is not the owner of goods, but is in possession of them, to retain them pending payment of a debt. For example, if a man takes his motor car into a garage for repair, the garage proprietor is entitled to keep it until his work is paid for.)

Section 25 (1): 'Where a person having ... agreed to buy goods, obtains, with the consent of the seller, possession of the goods ... the delivery or transfer by that person ... of the goods or documents of title under any sale, pledge or other disposition thereof to any person receiving the same in good faith and without notice of any lien or other right of the original seller in respect of the goods, has the same effect as if the person making the delivery or transfer were a mercantile agent in possession of the goods or documents of title with the consent of the owner.'

The sub-section 2 excludes from the operation of this provision a conditional sales (which is the position where there is retention of title by the original seller), which amounts to a consumer credit agreement for the purposes of the Consumer Credit Act 1974.

The term 'mercantile agent' is defined in section 26, but the effect of the section is that the sub-purchaser obtains a good title to the goods as though the delivery or transfer of the goods or documents of title to him were made with the consent of the original seller, the owner.

Where goods are admixed with others so that an ownership in common is created, section 25 (1) will only apply if the 'consent' with which the sub-purchaser is in possession of the goods is the consent of *all* the owners: *Lloyds Bank Ltd* v. *Bank of America* (1938).

'Possession with consent' for the purposes of section 25 (1) is sufficient even if the consent is obtained by fraud: *Du Jardin* v. *Beadman Bros. Ltd* (1952). But it is uncertain whether 'possession' means possession solely in connection with the seller/buyer relationship or whether possession for a purpose entirely unrelated to a transaction of that nature is covered. It is inconceivable that if Tom agrees to buy a car from Harry on the understanding that possession and title are not to pass until payment in cash has been made, and then Tom borrows the car from Harry in order to go to his bank to collect the money but disappears with it, Tom can defeat the true owner's title by selling it to an innocent purchaser.

It should be noted that for section 25 (1) of the Sale of Goods Act 1979 to operate there must be delivery or transfer *by way of sale* etc. Neither a receiver nor a liquidator can obtain title to the goods by virtue of this section. The word 'delivery' is defined in section 61 as meaning 'voluntary transfer of possession from one person to another'. Therefore a receiver or liquidator on appointment does not take 'delivery' within the meaning of section 61.

A person who has taken goods which are subject to retention of title clause or other condition is a person who has agreed to buy: *Lee* v. *Butler* (1893); *Marten* v. *Whale* (1917).

But the wording of section 25 (1) appears to be wide enough to cover the situation where a buyer in possession with a retention of title clause in favour of the true owners, sells and delivers to a sub-purchaser.

4.13 Sub-purchaser in good faith

Section 25 (1) only confers title where the sub-purchaser is one:

'... receiving the same in good faith and without notice of any lien *or other right* of the original sellers ....'

The Irish case of *In the matter of Interview Ltd* (1973) held on the Sale of Goods Act, 1893 that where a sub-purchaser knew that his seller had the goods subject to a retention of title clause by the original seller, he did not buy in good faith so as to get title. Mr Justice Kenny said:

'The effect of [the retention of title clause] was that the ownership and property in the goods remained in the German companies until the goods had been paid for. Thus [the buyers] could transfer the property and ownership in the goods to any person who bought them in good faith and without notice of the claim and right of the German companies....'

He then referred to the statute and section 9 of the Factors Act, 1889 and concluded,

'Interview cannot rely on the Act of 1889 or the Act of 1893 to validate the transaction as a sale because they did not receive the goods in good faith and they had notice of the rights of the original sellers, the German companies, in respect of the goods.'

It is submitted that the judgment in that case is correct on that point (but on that point alone).

A sub-purchaser who knows of the retention of title clause in favour of the original seller cannot therefore obtain a good title under this section from a buyer selling with or without the consent of the owner.

Chapter 5

Supply of Goods and Materials to the Construction Industry

5.01   Sub-contractors in the construction industry
The supply of materials and goods for building and similar work presents special problems for suppliers who seek to retain title until payment. To start with many, if not most, of the contracts which have as their object the supply of goods for construction work are contracts for work and materials and not sale of goods.

The common law provisions which existed before the codification in the Sale of Goods Act, 1893, that Act itself, and the current Sale of Goods Act 1979 have no application to these transactions. The distinction was emphasised by the Statute of Frauds 1677, section 17, which later became section 4 of the Sale of Goods Act, 1893, and was not repealed until the Law Reform (Enforcement of Contracts) Act, 1954, came into force.

Under the Statute of Frauds and section 4 of the 1893 Act, contracts for the sale of goods of the value of £10 or more had to be evidenced in writing before they could be enforced: contracts for goods and work were not subject to this provision. If a lift for a building were ordered then the contract would be unenforceable unless it was in writing; if a lift were ordered to be installed by the makers then the contract would be enforceable even though it was entirely oral.

For nearly three hundred years, therefore, there was a sharp distinction drawn between contracts for the sale of goods and contracts for the supply of work and materials and a vast amount of erudition has been dedicated to elucidating this distinction. Not all of this learning would commend itself to logicians. Why the making and supply of false teeth should be regarded as a sale of goods, but the making and supply of a portrait is a contract for work and material is not immediately apparent to the simple mind, but that is what has been decided by the courts: *Lee* v. *Griffin* (1861); *Robinson* v. *Graves* (1935).

Nor is it immediately apparent why the serving of a meal in a restaurant is the sale of goods and putting a hair dye on a customer is work and materials: *Lockett* v. *Charles* (1938); *Watson* v. *Buckley, Osborne, Garrett and Co. Ltd* (1940).

5.02   Sale of goods or work and materials?

Although this part of the Statute of Frauds was repealed in 1954, important consequences still flow from this distinction. For one thing, the implied terms of sections 13 and 14 of the Sale of Goods Act as to merchantable quality, fitness for purpose, etc. do not apply to contracts for work and materials and it is only within recent years that the courts have been willing to imply similar conditions where the supplier works with the materials he supplies. The illogicality of this was stressed by Mr Justice Hallett in the case of *Dodd and Dodd* v. *Wilson and McWilliam* (1946) where veterinary surgeons innoculated the plaintiff's cattle with an injection which injured them:

'It seems to me that justice certainly does not require that, by taking on themselves the administration of the substance in addition to recommending and supplying it, the defendants thereby in some way succeed in lessening their liability. It might, of course, increase their liability if their method of administration were improper ... but how can it lessen it?'

In the construction industry case of *Young & Marten Ltd* v. *McManus Childs Ltd* (1968) Lord Upjohn also criticised the distinction that appeared to exist between the obligation of a seller of goods and the supplier of them under a work and materials contract. It was, he said, 'most unsatisfactory, illogical and indeed a severe blow to any idea of a coherent system of law...'.

In that case, the House of Lords implied similar terms in a contractor's roofing contract to those in the Sale of Goods Act when the tiles proved to have a latent defect. The House of Lords has since extended this obligation further to cover both work and materials in *I.B.A.* v. *E.M.I. and B.I.C.C.* (1981).

Equally important is the fact that where a supplier is nominated by the architect, and that supplier is to provide goods for the contractor to fix to the building, it is regarded as a sale of goods by the supplier to the contractor; the ordinary rules for the passing of title therefore apply.

However, where the supplier is to do work as well as supply materials, since this is not the sale of goods, there is no intention that the property in the goods shall ever vest in the contractor. Frequently there is no contractual relationship between the employer (the building owner) and a sub-contractor, and even if there is, there is rarely any specific provision regarding the vesting of title in the employer.

The consequences can be seen from the case of *Dawby Williamson Roofing Ltd* v. *Humberside County Council* (1979). Humberside County Council entered into a contract with the main contractor for the erection of a school in the standard form of building contract, the Joint Contracts Tribunal (JCT) version of 1963. Roofing work was to be done by the plaintiff company as sub-contractors of the main contractors. These sub-contractors were not nominated by the Council or its architect and the contract they (the sub-contractors) entered into with the main contractor was in the form of contract known as the National Federation of Building Trades Employers/Federation of Associations of Specialists and Sub-contractors' 'blue form'. That contract made no specific provision for the passing of title in the materials but merely provided that 'the Sub-Contractor shall execute and complete the Sub-Contract works to the reasonable satisfaction of the Contractor' (clause 2). It also provided that nothing in the sub-contract should create any privity of contract between the sub-contractor and the employer (clause 3). The sub-contractor was to be responsible for loss or damage to any materials on site for the sub-contractor's use until 'such materials and goods have been fully, finally and properly incorporated into the works'.

In November 1976 the plaintiffs delivered to the site for use in their roofing work sixteen tons of Welsh roofing slates. Under the main contract clause 30 (2) of the 1963 edition, the architect was obliged to include in his interim certificates not only the value of work properly executed, but also 'of the materials and goods delivered to ... the Works for use thereon ...'. Clause 14 (1) further provided that where 'material or goods have ... been included in any interim certificate under which the contractor has received payment, such materials and goods all become the property of the Employer'. (Clause 16 of the 1980 edition of the JCT standard form of building contract contains similar provisions.)

The value of the sixteen tons of Welsh roofing slates brought on site by the sub-contractors was included in an interim certificate which was paid to the contractor. In January 1977 the contractors went into liquidation. This, under the contracts, had the effect of determining the sub-contractor's contract.

The sub-contractors received no payment for the slates and attempted to collect them. Humberside County Council refused to allow them to do so and subsequently made use of the slates for roofing the school, claiming that they were their property.

To whom did the slates belong?

It is surprising that a dispute of this nature ever reached the High Court, since the answer to this question was so simple as to be elementary: the slates remained the property of the roofing sub-contractor, Dawby Williamson Roofing Ltd. That company had not sold them to the main contractor and had never intended to do so. Therefore the contractor had no title he could pass to the employer, no matter what his contract might say. *Nemo dat quod non habet* [4.01].

Moreover, the sub-contractors were not a party to the JCT contract and there was no privity of contract of any kind between them and the employers. So that they were in no way bound by the terms of a contract to which they were not parties, even if they knew of its terms: *Scruttons* v. *Midland Silicones Ltd* (1962). It was argued, implausibly, that because by their contract with the contractor they were to be deemed to have knowledge of the terms of the JCT contract between the contractor and the employer, the terms of that contract were incorporated in their own by reference. The judge rejected this contention.

The NFBTE/FASS 'blue form' for non-nominated sub-contractors made the position perfectly clear, as did the 'green form' for nominated sub-contractors: 'Nothing on this Sub-Contract contained shall ... create any privity of contract between the Sub-Contractor and the Employer...' (the proviso to clause 3). The same words appear in NSC/4, for use with the JCT 80 contract (which replaces the 'green form'), in clause 5.2.

It is instructive to consider what the situation would have been if the plaintiffs had been simply suppliers of goods to the contractor. In the absence of any terms or indication to the contrary, the property would pass to the buyer, the contractor, either with the contract, if the goods were specific and identified, or at latest on delivery. The contractor could therefore pass a good title to the employer on payment of the interim certificate, by virtue of clause 14 of the JCT 63 contract.

Had the supplier retained title until he was paid, the contractor would be 'a person having ... agreed to buy goods' who had obtained 'with the consent of the seller, possession of the goods' for the purposes of section 25 (2) of the Sale of Goods Act, 1893. But it is doubtful whether the employer would have been the person to whom delivery was made, and if he, or his agent the architect, knew that the original seller had retained title, the property would not pass under that section (25 (1) of the 1979 Act). The supplier would therefore still be the owner of the tiles. Even if property did pass, on the tracing principle the sum of money received by the contractor would be impressed with the sub-contractor's rights in the hands of the liquidator.

From the above it will be seen that in law there is still an important question to be answered: whether a supplier provides materials under a contract of sale or whether he supplies and instals them, in which case it will be a contract of work and materials.

5.03 The distinction between sale and work and materials

It is not always easy to distinguish between the two in law, as the cases mentioned earlier make clear. But it may be vital. In Australia it has been held that a contract for the supply and installation of a revolving cocktail cabinet which slotted into fastenings on the floor and ceiling was a contract for work and materials: *Brooks Robinson Pty Ltd* v. *Rothfield* (1951). So also were seats installed in a lecture theatre: *Aristoc Industries* v. *R.A. Wenham (Builders) Pty Ltd* (1965), and a lift installed in a building: *Sydney Hydraulic & General Engineering* v. *Blackwood* (1908). On the other hand the installation of a domestic heater was held to be a contract of sale: *Collins Trading* v. *Maher* (1969).

In England, it has been held that where the method of installation is a minor part of the work the contract is for the sale of goods, so that fitted carpets come in this category: *Philip Head & Co.* v. *Shopfronts Ltd* (1970).

Formerly, it was said that when 'the contract is such that a chattel is ultimately to be delivered ... the cause of action is goods sold and delivered': *Lee* v. *Griffin* (1861). But that is no longer a reliable test, and there can be little doubt that if the contract requires the design, fabrication and installation in a building of an air-conditioning plant, for example, it will be a contract for work and materials.

5.04   Affixtures to the realty

Retention of title on building and construction materials is further complicated by the principle that chattels which become permanently affixed to the realty cease to exist as chattels and become part of the land.

Mr Justice Blackburn in *Holland* v. *Hodgson* (1872) said:

There is no doubt *quicquid plantatur solo, solo cedit:* that the general maxim of the law is that what is annexed to the land becomes part of the land ....'

But the learned judge had to qualify that observation by further comment:

'When the article in question is no further attached to the land than by its own weight it is generally considered to be a chattel. But even in such a case, if the intention is apparent to make the articles part of the land, they then become part of the land.

'On the other hand, an article may be firmly affixed to the land and yet the circumstances may be such that it was never intended to be part of the land and then it does not become part of the land.'

However, since most goods and materials supplied to a construction site are both securely affixed and intended to become part of the land, as a matter of principle they cease to exist as chattels as soon as they are fixed. A seller with a retention of title clause will therefore have his rights to reclaim the goods defeated as soon as those goods become part of the building, subject to the principles set out below. This will apply not only to such obvious goods and materials as cement or paint but also to substantial plant such as lifts, air-conditioning plants, and boilers and heaters.

In theory, this general legal position resulting from the common law can be altered by contractual obligations to the contrary. It is open to a supplier of doors, for example, to stipulate that he retains title until payment and that should the contractor to whom he has supplied them have a receiver appointed or go into liquidation, he shall be entitled to enter on the site to remove the doors whether or not they are affixed to the realty. There is no reason, it is thought, why that should not be a valid term *inter partes,* i.e. between the contractor and the supplier, but the difficulty from the point of the supplier is that there is normally no contractual relationship between himself and the employer, the owner of the building, and the licence to enter would come to an end the moment the contractor ceased to be in possession of the site — as, under the standard contracts, he does in the event of receivership or insolvency. The fact that the contractor has agreed to the removal of doors from the realty can in no way bind the owner of the building. If the owner of the building ordered the doors on those terms, it would probably be binding on him but the courts have shown little inclination to enforce similar agreements where machinery on hire-purchase has been affixed to the realty.

In *Hobson* v. *Gorringe* (1897), it was held that the owner of goods supplied on hire purchase was entitled to enter on the land and remove his goods which had been affixed to the realty. The terms of hire purchase agreement constituted a licence, coupled with an interest in the land.

But it would seem that this right is limited.

It will defeat a debenture holder with a floating charge created *after* the hire purchase agreement. The right to enter and recover the goods, even affixed goods, takes priority over subsequently created equitable interests, whether the debenture holders are aware of the hire purchase agreement or not: *re Morrison Jones & Taylor Ltd* (1914).

It will not defeat a debenture holder with a legal mortgage of land created after the agreement who has no notice of the hire purchase agreement.

In the case of goods brought on and affixed to the realty after a specific mortgage of land, whether legal or equitable, has been created, these goods become part of the mortgagee's security, even if the mortgagee knew of the agreement: *Longbottom* v. *Berry* (1869); *Meux* v. *Jacobs* (1875). But if there is a floating charge over a company's assets which does not specifically attach to the land until it has crystallised, an owner of goods can remove his affixed goods before the charge has crystallised and if he does so, the charge does not exist over his goods: *re Morrison Jones and Taylor Ltd (supra)*.

Plant and business fixtures may readily be presumed as excluded from mortgages and charges over realty by agreement between a company and debenture holders: *Gough* v. *Wood & Co.* (1894).

The position of unpaid sellers who have retained title and whose goods have been affixed to the realty will be identical in all respects with those who own and let out goods on hire purchase agreements.

5.05   Retention and the Joint Contracts Tribunal

In 1978, the Joint Contract Tribunal, the body which is responsible for drafting the Standard Form of Building Contract, issued a formal notice entitled 'Retention of title (ownership) by suppliers of building material and goods'.

'The joint Contracts Tribunal announces that, through its constituent bodies, it has been informed of the following problem: Some suppliers of building materials and goods are including provisions in their contracts of sale with contractors and subcontractors under which the supplier retains ownership of such goods and materials after their delivery to the site. The terms on which such retention of ownership is secured appear to vary; but in many cases the passing of ownership to a contractor or sub-contractor is dependent upon payment in full for the relevant materials and goods. It is understood that suppliers anticipate being able to use such provisions to enable them either to re-possess the goods and materials if they have not been paid for in full; or to claim against the proceeds of any re-sale.

Some employers (and their professional advisers) are seeking to obtain proof of ownership by the contractor (or through the contractor, by any relevant sub-contractor) before operating the provisions of Clause 30 (2) [of the 1963 JCT form]. Moreover in current tenders some employers are seeking to amend Clause 30 (2) by making it a condition of the operation of the valuation provisions in that sub-clause that the contractor provides proof of ownership.

The tribunal has considered this matter to see if there is sufficient substance for the concern being expressed by some employers (and their professional advisers) to justify any change in the existing Standard Form provisions in Clause 30 (2) and in Clause 14 (1). The tribunal, with the concurrence of its constituent bodies, does not think that any change is desirable and the main reasons for reaching this decision are set out below:

Reasons for decision by Tribunal not to amend Clause 30 (2) and Clause 14 (1)

(1) A requirement on the contractor to prove ownership of on-site materials and goods could raise serious legal problems, both for the contractor, any relevant sub-contractors and also for the employer (and his professional advisers). Such a requirement would, therefore, be difficult to meet and so might mean, in practice, that payment for on-site goods and materials would not be operated. Moreover, the obtaining of proof of ownership would add to administration costs as would the checking of such proof by, or on behalf of, the employer. The tribunal concluded that such a requirement would add to the costs of building work by reason of additional administration; and might cause tender prices to rise because contractors and sub-contractors could no longer be certain that materials and goods properly on site would be valued and paid for in interim certificates.

(2) The degree of risk to the employer from not obtaining proof of ownership before paying for on-site goods and materials in interim certificates was not considered sufficiently great to justify the possible additional costs, referred to in (1) above for the following reasons:

(a) The period of risk runs only until such time as the on-site goods and materials are incorporated in the Works; from the time of incorporation they cease to be chattels, and any right to re-possess by a supplier would be lost. The period of risk is, therefore, from the date of payment by the employer of the relevant interim certificates to the time at which the relevant goods and materials are incorporated in the Works. This is unlikely to be more than a relatively short period.

(b) During the limited period referred to in (a), the risk of re-possession by a supplier would only, in practice, arise if a main contractor became insolvent. Such insolvency occurs only on a small proportion of the total number of building contracts and this reduces the degree of risk even further.

(c) The tribunal understands that in many cases the supply contract permits the contractor or sub-contractor to re-sell the goods and materials. In such cases the supplier's rights are against the proceeds of re-sale and the supplier has no right to re-possess the goods and materials. This reduces the risk to the employer still further.'

5.06   The position of an architect or engineer when certifying
That statement by the Joint Contracts Tribunal merits some comment.

An architect or engineer who is called upon to certify the value of goods supplied or work done for an interim or final certificate under any building contract is liable in contract and in tort to his employer for negligent over-ceritification: *Sutcliffe* v. *Thackrah* (1974). He is also liable to the contractor in tort for negligent under-certification: *Stevenson* v. *Watson* (1879). Although the Court of Appeal decided in the case of *Chambers* v. *Goldthorpe* (1901) that an architect issuing a final certificate was a 'quasi-arbitrator' and therefore protected from an action by employer or builder for negligent certification, the House of Lords in *Sutcliffe* v. *Thackrah* (1974) overthrew this principle, although it had been accepted for more than seventy years and was described by Lord Radcliffe in the House of Lords in *R. B. Burden* v. *Swansea Corporation* (1957) as 'established law'. As a result, an architect or engineer who issues a certificate for interim or final payments under a construction contract is not protected in any way for negligent certification.

It is self-evident that he must be liable to his employer if he issues a certificate to the contractor for payment of on-site goods without satisfying himself that the contractor can pass such a title to the employer as will make the employer the owner of the goods for which he has to pay.

In the case of *Ashwell Scott Ltd* v. *Eastlease Ltd* (1980) the plaintiffs secured, with a tender of £624,339, a contract for the construction and equipment of a new computer centre on the Bride Kiln Industrial Estate at Milton Keynes for Scientific Control Systems Ltd ('Scicon'). They started work in April 1973 on the basis of a 'letter of intent' but the contract, in the terms of the Model Conditions of the Institute of Mechanical and Electrical Engineers (1966 edition) was not signed until 2 July 1973.

The Milton Keynes Development Corporation undertook to act as 'architects, surveyors and engineers' for the project, as agents for Scicon.

On 21 October 1973 they gave Ashwell Scott seven days notice to get off the site, which was complied with. The contractor therefore, in a case named *Ashwell Scott Ltd* v. *Scientific Control Systems Ltd; Milton Keynes Development Corporation, Third Party* (1979) sued for damages for breach of contract and for a *quantum meruit* for work done and materials supplied of £327,033. Scicon brought in the Development Corporation, their 'architects, surveyors and engineers' as a third party and claimed a full indemnity should they be found liable.

After a sixteen-day hearing of that case, Judge Fay Q.C. ruled on three preliminary points. He held that the expulsion of Ashwell Scott from the site was not a valid exercise of the power to determine the contract contained in clause 12 of the Model Conditions. He held that Ashwell Scott had not repudiated the contract. He also held that by their expulsion from the site Scientific Control Systems Ltd had been guilty of a wrongful repudiation of the contract.

In the course of the hearing, it emerged that there was an ingenious arrangement between all the parties whereby the air-conditioning to be installed was leased from Eastlease Ltd, the leasing subsidiary of the Norwich Union, with the benefit of 100% write-off against corporation taxation as 'plant', while at the same time constituting 'new build' and therefore zero-rated for the purposes of VAT. At the same time, the engineer was to include it in certificates he issued to Scicon for payment to the contractors.

Questions about the ownership of those goods were canvassed in front of the judge, and the effect of sections 25 (1) of the Sale of Goods Act, 1893, the Finance Acts and the Bills of Sale Act were all discussed. He decided that title had passed by estoppel when the air-conditioning was incorporated in the building on the analogy of section 21 (1) of the Sale of Goods Act, 1893.

He held there had been no binding contract whereby Eastlease Ltd had undertaken to buy the goods from Ashwell Scott.

'The arrangement made ... related only to the mode of payment of Scicon's debts.'

It was in connection with this that he made the remark:

'An engineer who includes in a certificate goods which are not the property of the contractor does so at his own peril.'

In the particular circumstances of this case, no doubt the employer would be estopped from complaining that the engineer in issuing certificates for goods, the title for which he well knew was not intended to pass to his employer, was negligent. And, of course, the judge held that the property *had* passed when the air-conditioning became incorporated in the realty.

However, the architect who included the slates in his interim certificate in *Dawby Williamson Ltd* v. *Humberside ·County Council* [5.00] could have no such defence.

It is not surprising therefore that architects are unwilling to include goods brought on site in interim certificates without proof that the contractor can pass ownership of the goods to the employer. Clearly they do so at their peril, if the contractor should become insolvent before the goods are affixed.

5.07   The standard form of building contract JCT 80: suppliers
The 1980 version of the Joint Contracts Tribunal's standard form (still known to some judges as 'the RIBA contract', in spite of a direction in 1977 in *Court Business,* item B.586, that it should be otherwise described) gives a restricted meaning to nominated suppliers.

By clause 36.1.2, it does not apply unless there has been a prime cost sum in the bill of quantities for these goods or materials – even though the supplier has been named in the bills or there is a sole supplier of such goods or materials.

Clause 36.4 prevents an architect nominating any supplier unless that supplier is willing to enter into a contract with the main contractor, on a contract which contains eleven terms. One of these is clause 36.4.7 and reads 'that the ownership of materials or goods shall pass to the Contractor upon delivery by the Nominated Supplier ... whether or not payment has been made in full'.

It will be observed that this clause interferes with normal English provisions as to passing of title contained in rule 1 of section 18 of the Sale of Goods Act 1979. That rule reads:

'Where there is an unconditional contract for the sale of specific goods in a deliverable state, the property in the goods passes to the buyer when the contract is made and it is immaterial whether the time of payment or the time of delivery, or both, be postponed.'

Clause 36 substitutes for that passage of title upon delivery. The supplier and the contractor can, of course, displace rule 1 or any other rule by a specific agreement to the contrary. But it would require the agreement of both parties and it would not be effected by an order to deliver say, ten thousand bricks to the site. In that case property will pass not upon delivery but when, in accordance with rule 3, the seller has set aside this quantity of bricks and 'the buyer has notice thereof'. The latter, of course, may be when the bricks arrive at the site but it will not be a term of the contract.

Clause 36.4 expressly exempts from the provision that the contractor shall only be obliged to accept nominated suppliers who enter into a contract on the specified terms 'where the architect and contractor shall otherwise agree'. The architect, as agent of the employer in this context, has no power to vary the terms of the contract.

The terms of the contract are silent about what happens if the contractor, through inadvertance or otherwise, accepts the nomination of a supplier who insists on retaining title until payment has been made and who is not willing to enter into a contract whereby the property shall pass upon delivery. The contractor clearly will be bound by the contract he has entered into with the supplier.

All clause 36.4 does is to give him the right to reject a nomination where the supplier retains title until payment. If he accepts it, he will be bound by it.

5.08   The standard form of building contract JCT 80: sub-contractors

There are other forms for use with the standard form of contract between the employer and the main contractor.

What is termed the 'basic method' of appointing sub-contractors is set out in clause 35 of JCT 80. This involves the use of a newly-drafted contractual document known as NSC/2 between the employer and the sub-contractor, *before* the sub-contractor has been formally nominated. It authorises the architect to order the sub-contractor before nomination to design and manufacture materials and goods for the works. If the sub-contractor does not get the nomination, the employer undertakes to pay for the design and materials and 'upon such payment such materials and goods shall become the property of the employer'.

This is the only reference to the passing of title to the goods and the contract is silent as to when property shall pass if the sub-contractor succeeds in becoming nominated. Presumably, it is only on affixture to the realty.

If he is nominated, he is required to enter into a contract with the contractor in the form NSC/4, which replaces the form NFBTE/FASS 'green form' used with JCT 63.

As with the green form, it specifies that nothing contained in the sub-contract documents shall be so construed as to 'create any privity of contract between the sub-contractor and the employer':

Clause 5.2.

The main JCT 80 contract retains the provisions in clause 30.2 which requires the architect to include in his interim certificates not only work properly executed by the sub-contractor but also (by 21.4.12 of NSC/4) 'the total value of the materials and goods delivered to or adjacent to the works for incorporation therein by the sub-contractor...'. Clause 16.1 of JCT 80 again provides that where such material or goods are included in an interim certificate and paid for 'such materials and goods shall become the property of the employer'.

Once again this clause is totally ineffective to pass title to the employer. In the case of sub-contractors providing work and materials, the main contractor has no title to pass to the employer and the sub-contractor is not a party to the JCT 80 form containing these provisions. As in *Dawby Williamson* [5.02], the property in goods and materials brought on site by the sub-contractor, if he actually owns them, remains vested in him until he incorporates them in the building — even if the main contractor has been paid for them. No doubt, if the sub-contractor actually receives payment for them before they are incorporated, the courts would readily assume, in spite of the curious silence of the contract NSC/4 and 4a about this, that it was the intention of the parties that property should pass to the employer.

5.09 Materials off-site
The JCT 80 standard form empowers, but does not require, the architect to include in an interim certificate the value of any materials or goods 'before delivery thereof to or adjacent to the Works' provided they are materials intended for incorporation (clause 30.3).

There are a number of conditions which circumscribe this discretion of the architect but the most material ones for present purposes are:

Clause 30.3.4: 'where the materials were ordered from a supplier by the Contractor or by any sub-contractor, the contract for their supply is in writing and expressly provides that the property therein shall pass unconditionally to the Contractor or sub-contractor....'

Clause 30.3.5: 'where the materials were ordered from a supplier by any sub-contractor, the relevant sub-contract between the Contractor and the sub-contractor is in writing and expressly provides that on the property in the material passing to the sub-contractor the same shall immediately pass to the contractor.'

Clause 30.3.6: 'where the materials were manufactured or assembled by any sub-contractor, the sub-contract is in writing and expressly provides that the property in the materials shall pass unconditionally to the contractor.'

These clauses are specifically aimed at preventing the architect from including in his interim certificates materials off-site for which the original supplier has retained title until payment.

Curiously, these clauses would appear to exclude the architect from including in interim certificates off-site material prepared or obtained by a nominated sub-contractor under 'the basic method', NSC/4, or the 'alternative method', NSC/4a, since neither of these contracts provides that property in the goods shall ever pass to the contractor.

A further requisite before the architect may include off-site goods or materials in any interim certificate is:

Clause 30.3.8: 'the Contractor provides the Architect ... with reasonable proof that the property in the materials is in him and that the appropriate conditions set out in clauses 30.3.1 to 30.3.1.7 have been complied with.'

This being so, it seems strange that the provision in clause 30.3 appears at all in the contract since there can rarely be cases where the condition can be complied with. The clause corresponds roughly to clause 30 (2A), incorporated at a late stage into the JCT 63 contract.

5.10   Other contracts

The JCT 80 standard form of building contract is not the only form in use for building work in the United Kingdom. For work by government departments, it is common to use the GC/Works/1 form devised by the Property Services Agency of the Department of Environment. Civil engineering work is usually done under the fifth edition of the Institution of Civil Engineers (ICE) contract.

Neither of these has, as yet, made specific provision for the effect of retention of title clauses so they will be governed by the principles set out above for the standard form.

Re Yorkshire Joinery Co (1967) 111 Sol J 701 — building matls part of factory & unpaid vendors unable rely on retainshn of title .

Chapter 6

Insolvency and Retention Clauses

6.01 The difference between bankruptcy and liquidation

Although it is common in ordinary speech to refer to a limited company as being 'bankrupt', in law only individuals or partnerships can become bankrupt. Insolvent companies are put into liquidation. A receiver can be appointed to a company which is not insolvent and receivership is not followed inevitably by liquidation.

Since most business transactions take place these days between limited companies, bankruptcy is here treated only in outline. It is a process of law whereby the property of a debtor is taken over by a person appointed by the court, called the trustee in bankruptcy, for distribution amongst his creditors.

The Bankruptcy Act, 1914, sections 1 and 107, specify a number of 'available acts of bankruptcy' but other statutes provide further 'acts' (see Administration of Justice Act 1965, Attachment of Earnings Act 1971, and Criminal Justice Act 1972). These 'available acts' can trigger off the procedure whereby a person is made bankrupt.

Most persons are the subject of bankruptcy proceedings as the result of failure to comply with a formal 'bankruptcy notice' served by a creditor who has an unsatisfied court judgment against the debtor. Another common ground is where the creditor himself petitions on the ground of his own insolvency.

6.02   The effect of receiving orders

If a bankruptcy petition has been proved, the court makes a receiving order whereby the Official Receiver, a Department of Trade official, is empowered to deal with all the debtor's assets.

The receiving order does not make the debtor bankrupt, nor does it divest him of his property. It merely deprives him of the power of disposing of his property, or in the case of a partnership, of any of the firm's property (Bankruptcy Act, 1914, section 7). It has the effect of stopping any further legal actions being brought against the debtor in respect of any debt provable in the bankruptcy. It will not, however, stop actions (e.g. in tort) for unliquidated damages, since these are not, until judgement, provable in the bankruptcy.

More important for our present purpose is that it does not affect the rights of a secured creditor (Bankruptcy Act, 1914, section 7 (2)).

A secured creditor is any person who holds a mortgage, charge or lien on the debtor's property of any kind as security for a debt.

So far as goods are in the possession of a person subject to a receiving order and those goods are subject to a valid retention of title clause, they do not pass into the power of the Official Receiver.

If however the retention of title clause confers no more than a legal or equitable charge on the goods, the creditor is a secured creditor and can, notwithstanding the receiving order, proceed to exercise such rights as he is given by the terms of his security.

A secured creditor can realise his security without obtaining judgment or presenting a bankruptcy petition. But if a secured creditor presents the petition, the alternative in the petition is put to him of either offering to surrender his security in favour of creditors generally, so that he will rank with the unsecured creditors, or valuing his security in cash terms (Bankruptcy Act, 1914, section 4 (2)). If he elects to do the latter, he will be a petitioning creditor only in respect of any debt in excess of the estimated value of his security.

Nothing in a receiving order will prevent a seller reclaiming goods subject to a retention of title clause from the person against whom such an order has been made, or from the Official Receiver. Nor will it interfere with the right of a seller, who has only a charge against the goods, from exercising a right of recovery of the goods if the contract so provides.

But it is prudent to include in any retention terms an express provision that the right of the purchaser to possession of the goods shall cease if a receiving order is made against him. Such a right will not automatically, in the absence of an express term, authorise an unpaid seller to enter upon premises to recover his goods, and it is therefore desirable to incorporate as well an express licence to do so.

Prompt action on notice of a receiving order is essential, for reasons which will become apparent later.

6.03   The position of the Official Receiver under a receiving order
The receiving order in no way transfers any of the debtor's property, real or personal, to the Official Receiver: *Rhodes* v. *Dawson* (1886).

'A receiving order is not equivalent to an adjudication of bankruptcy. It does not divest the debtor of his property, nor make him a bankrupt, nor place him under the disabilities of an adjudicated bankrupt. Notwithstanding a receiving order, the debtor is the only person who can sue for the recovery of what belongs to him. What the plaintiff recovers is his property both legally and equitably, although he must, when he recovers it, hand it over to the Official Receiver for the benefit of his creditors if he does not pay or compound with them...' (per Lord Justice Lindley).

The Official Receiver has no power to dispose of any goods in the possession of the debtor. He is there solely to preserve and protect them. The sole exception to this rule is perishable goods (Bankruptcy Act 1914, section 74 (2)).

It follows therefore that the Official Receiver has no power to sell or otherwise dispose of goods in the debtor's possession that are not his property because they are subject to a retention of title clause. Still less, has he the power to sell goods subject to a charge, whether this has been registered under the Bills of Sale Acts or not.

But if the debtor wishes to dispose of such goods after a receiving order has been made, he can only do so with the consent of the Official Receiver.

The Official Receiver has power to take possession of the debtor's premises with the rest of his property. But he acquires no title to them, or legal or equitable interest in them, and as a matter of law the debtor remains the occupier: *re Smith, ex parte Mason* (1893). A receiving order having been made against one James Smith, who carried on a substantial business in Brixton, the gas company, under statutory clauses, cut off the supply of gas to the premises. By the statutes then current, gas companies were obliged to supply gas on the application of 'an owner or occupier' of premises. They refused to reconnect the gas supply for the Official Receiver. It was held by Mr Justice Vaughan Williams that the Official Receiver was not the occupier of the premises but the debtor still was:

'It is plain that the receiver could not claim a supply of gas as 'occupier' here, unless he was in a position to say that the occupation of the debtor had come to an end.

'It seems to me quite plain that the occupation of the debtor had not come to an end.

'The case of *Rhodes* v. *Dawson* shows that his estate is unaltered by the making of the receiving order. The same premises continue to be vested in him that were vested in him before the making of the receiving order ....

'It was suggested that, though the premises might still be vested in him, the contract had been put to an end by the making of the receiving order...'.

His lordship dismissed that proposition, and said,

'The estate remains the same, and the contract remains the same ... and the occupation of the debtor remains the same.'

From this it follows that the Official Receiver is subject to all the contractual rights of a seller who has retained title. If he sells goods belonging to an unpaid seller which are in the possession of the debtor, he commits the tort of conversion (also called 'trover') which is now subject to the provisions of the Torts (Inference with Goods) Act 1977. He is personally liable. He has no power, even if he is in possession of a debtor's premises, to refuse to allow the owner of goods on the premises to enter and reclaim his property if such a right has been granted by the debtor in his contract with the seller.

The position of the debtor is, however, radically altered if he is adjudicated bankrupt; and with it the rights of a seller who has retained title.

6.04 The effect of adjudication

If the debtor is unable to satisfy his creditors in full or reach an accommodation with them by way of a composition which the court approves, the next step in the bankruptcy proceedings is the adjudication of the debtor as a bankrupt.

The Official Receiver then calls a meeting of creditors, interviews the debtor and requires him to prepare a 'statement of affairs' and requires the debtor to attend court for a 'public examination'. The court is usually a county court with bankruptcy jurisdiction and in practice the registrar presides over the public examination.

The effect of an adjudication order made by the court is that the debtor is divested of all his property and the trustee in bankruptcy, if one has been appointed, automatically becomes the owner of it. The trustee in bankruptcy can be the Official Receiver, unless a separate trustee is nominated by the creditors and appointed by the court.

The trustee in bankruptcy has all the powers of an ordinary owner of property, save that he holds subject to a trust for the benefit of creditors, but there are certain things he cannot do except with the consent of a committee of inspection formed by the creditors. One of these is to carry on the bankrupt's business; another is to appoint a solicitor. With such consent, he can employ the bankrupt or make an allowance to him out of his assets. Where there is no committee of inspection, the trustee requires the consent of the Department of Trade.

Goods in the possession of the bankrupt, where the legal title has been retained by an unpaid seller, do not pass to a trustee of bankruptcy for the simple reason they are not the goods of the bankrupt. However, in some cases, the trustee may be titled to dispose of such goods for the benefit of the creditors in general under the doctrine of apparent (or reputed) ownership. The effect of this doctrine is to defeat completely the retention of title clause and to relegate the unpaid seller to the status of unsecured creditor.

This doctrine, it is said, has no application to limited liability companies: *Gorringe* v. *Irwell India Rubber & Gutta Percha Works* (1886). (It can be argued that this case was wrongly decided but the present author does not propose to set out the reasons, and it has stood as established law for nearly a century.)

6.05   Reputed ownership

If goods are in the 'possession, order or disposition' of the bankrupt, for the purposes of the bankrupt's business, with the consent of the owner, the bankrupt is deemed to be 'the reputed owner' of them. The result is that the trustee in bankruptcy can sell such goods and use the proceeds to satisfy the claims of the creditors.

This follows from the provisions of the Bankruptcy Act, 1914, section 38 (c), which reads:

Section 38: 'The property of the bankrupt divisible amongst his creditors ... shall comprise ...
(c)   all goods being, at the commencement of the bankruptcy, in the possession, order or disposition of the bankrupt, in his trade or business, by the consent and permission of the true owner, under such circumstances that he is the reputed owner thereof...'.

This reproduces similar provisions in bankruptcy statutes going back to the reign of James I, and the rationale for it was given by Lord Justice James in *ex parte Wingfield* (1879):

'It has always been construed as meaning this: that if goods are in a man's possession, order or disposition, under such circumstances as to enable him by means of them to obtain false credit, then the owner of the goods who permitted him to obtain that false credit is to suffer the penalty of losing his goods for the benefit of those who have given him credit.'

An immense amount of learning has accumulated around these fatuous provisions. In *re Fox* (1948), for example, it was held that building materials in the bankrupt contractor's yard were subject to the reputed ownership doctrine but those in his possession on site were not.

It is not proposed to discuss the cases here, except to point out that exactly the same reasoning would be applicable to goods in the possession of a limited liability company but, as has been pointed out, the doctrine has been held not to apply to companies. A retention of title clause in an agreement to sell to an individual or a partnership may therefore be defeated by these provisions, where it would not be in similar circumstances on supply to a limited liability company.

Where legal title passes on a sale of goods to an individual but equitable ownership is retained, the reputed ownership clause will not apply because of the provisions of section 38 (1) of the Bankruptcy Act, 1914; see also *Ryall* v. *Rolle* (1749), *Hollinshead* v. *Egan Ltd* (1913). Nor does it apply to goods in the possession of those who are in business as factors or mercantile agents: *Godfrey* v. *Furzo* (1733); or those in possession for a specified purpose: *re Brickwood* (1815).

A new section of the Bankruptcy Act, Section 38A, inserted by the Consumer Credit Act 1974, excludes application of the doctrine to goods 'agreed to be sold under a conditional sale agreement'. This might well have applied to all retention of title clauses, so to excluded goods supplied under them, but for a limited definition of the words 'conditional sale agreement'.

By section 38A (2) those words are defined as:

'... an agreement for the sale of goods under which the purchase price or part of it is payable by instalments and the property in the goods is to remain in the seller (notwithstanding that the buyer is to be in possession of the goods) until such conditions as to the payment of instalments or otherwise as may be specified in the agreement are fulfilled.'

On agreements to sell to private individuals or partnerships therefore, it would be prudent to insert in a retention of title clause that the purchase price should be payable by instalments.

The reputed ownership clause can also be defeated by evidence that goods of the description concerned are habitually in the possession of persons of that particular trade without them being the owners of them. There are numerous cases regarding this: an example is to be found in *re Lock* (1891) where the practice of manufacturers of safes in supplying retailers with them and retaining title was held to defeat the reputed ownership doctrine. If retention of title clauses continue to be as popular as they are at present, they may well deprive the section of its usefulness to a trustee in bankruptcy.

6.06   Title of a trustee in bankruptcy

By a legal fiction, the title of a trustee in bankruptcy is held to relate back to and to commence at the time when the 'available act of bankruptcy', on which the receiving order was made or any earlier act within three months before the order, took place (Bankruptcy Act, 1914, section 37).

This means, in effect, that the trustee has the right to nullify transactions which are in the nature of fraudulent preferences or other wrongful disposition of the bankrupt's assets. But bona fide transactions are valid (Bankruptcy Act, 1914, section 45).

6.07   Winding-up of companies

More than one third of the Companies Acts, 1948–1967, is concerned with the removal of companies from the register by way of winding-up. There are also voluminous regulations which are applicable, not to mention other enactments such as the Insolvency Act 1976 and the Insolvency Services (Accounting and Investment) Act 1970.

In essence, a company can be wound up in three different ways:

by the court;
under the supervision of the court;
voluntarily (Companies Act, 1948, sections 211–365).

The court concerned is normally the Chancery Division of the High Court, but where the share capital does not exceed £120,000, the county court for the district in which the registered office of the company is situated has concurrent jurisdiction (Companies Act, 1948, section 218 (as amended)).

The person in charge of the winding-up of a company, whether that company be wound up compulsorily or voluntarily is termed the 'liquidator'.

Secured creditors of the company invariably protect their security by taking the power to appoint a receiver. There can be such a thing as a debenture which does not give the debenture holder a charge over the company's assets, but normally a debenture will create a specific and floating charge over the company's assets and provide that, on the occurrence of certain events such as default on payment of interest by the company, the debenture holders may appoint a receiver. Mortgages also usually contain similar provisions.

This right can be exercised even though the company has gone into liquidation. If a receiver has not taken possession before a winding-up order has been made, such a receiver has to obtain leave of the court, but this is readily given and the court will not appoint the liquidator in his place: *re Henry Pound Son & Hitchin* (1889).

The court can also appoint a receiver in a wide variety of circumstances.

The appointment of a receiver has the effect of paralysing nearly all the powers of the directors of the company. All that is left to them is power to sign accounts and, in some circumstances, to affix the company seal.

6.08   The powers of a receiver

Apart from receivers appointed by the court, the powers of a receiver are not a matter of law but of contract. A receiver is limited to the powers conferred on him by the instrument under which he is appointed. His status is likewise determined, whether he is to be the agent of the debenture holders or the agent of the company. Invariably, for obvious reasons, he is made solely the agent of the company.

The Companies Act, 1948, section 369 (1) provides that:

'A receiver or manager of the property of a company appointed under the powers contained in any instrument may apply to the court for directions in relation to any particular matter arising in connection with the performance of his functions and on such application the court may give such directions, or may make such order declaring the rights of persons before the court or otherwise as the court thinks just.'

Questions regarding the effectiveness of retention of title clauses can be determined under this section by the court and it would appear that this can be so even if the owners of the goods are not parties to the action. Such proceedings are by way of originating summons.

The object of a receiver is to realise the company's assets so as to satisfy his own fees and expenses and the claims of the secured creditors. He is obliged to first satisfy the preferential creditors, except where the charge is over fixed assets. If so authorised by the court, or the instrument of appointment, he can carry on the business of the company as manager.

6.09   The position of a receiver

The assets of the company, however, do not vest in the receiver, although he has the power to realise them by sale.

He does not become a party to contracts in existence with the company, and it follows that he cannot vary such contracts.

In *Parsons* v. *Sovereign Bank of Canada* (1912), Parsons were merchants who had contracts for the supply of paper over three years with the Imperial Paper Mills Ltd. When those contracts had still two years to run, a receiver with power to manage the company, was appointed by the court at the instance of Sovereign Bank who held debentures in the company. The receiver purported to cancel the contracts at the time when Parsons owed $15,754 to the company. Parsons therefore deducted by way of set-off from this sum, damages for breach of contract. Discussing the appointment of a receiver, Lord Haldane said:

'The company remains in existence, but has lost its title to control its assets and its affairs....

'In the absence of a liquidation, the *persona* of the ... company remains legally intact though controlled by the receivers and managers....

'In the case of contracts to deliver paper ... there appears to be no reason for saying that the possession of the undertaking and the assets [by the receivers] ... put an end to these contracts. The company remained in legal existence and so did the contracts until put an end to otherwise.'

The court therefore held that the company, and therefore its assignees, the bank, could not sue for the price of paper delivered to Parsons except subject to Parsons counter-claim for damages. As these exceeded the amount of the claim, nothing was due to the company's assignees, the bank.

So, too in *George Barker Ltd* v. *Eynon* (1974). Lord Justice Edmund Davies, as he then was, said of the appointment of a receiver,

'He must fulfil company trading contracts entered into before his appointment or he renders it liable in damages if he unwarrantably declines to do so: see the authorities conveniently collected in *Buckley on the Companies Acts* 13th edition, (1957), page 244.

'Neither the receiver nor the debenture holders were in any way relieved by the former's appointment from the obligation which, by pre-appointment contracts, the company had undertaken.'

Consequently, the Court of Appeal held that the plaintiffs, a transport firm carrying meat for the company concerned, were entitled to a contractual lien over the goods carried, even after the appointment of the receiver.

Two things necessarily follow from this position of a receiver:

if the receiver takes possession of the assets of a company and he finds in possession of the company goods which remain, as the result of a retention of title clause, the property of the unpaid seller, he is subject to exactly the same contractual conditions as was the company. There can be no question of the debenture holders having any rights which rank in priority to those of the unpaid seller;

the receiver can only acquire title to the goods in exactly the same way the company can, i.e. by paying the full amount due to the seller.

It follows that a legal retention of title clause, which authorises the company to sell-on the goods and receive the rights to the proceeds of re-sale to the seller, is effective against a receiver and debenture holders.

6.10 Equitable rights of unpaid sellers
Moreover, any unpaid seller with only an equitable charge over the goods will take priority over a receiver and debenture holders,

whatever the nature or wording of the instrument by which the receiver was appointed.

In *Wilson* v. *Kelland* (1910), the Bedford Brewery (Plymouth) Ltd executed in 1901 a trust deed in favour of the Law Guarantee and Trust Society which was in effect a debenture with floating charge over all the company's assets, present and future, with a mortgage of specific properties. It provided that the brewery company 'shall not be at liberty to create any mortgage or charge on such premises ranking in priority to or in pari passu with the security created in favour of the debentures'.

Three years later in 1904, the company agreed to buy a brewery from A. and W. Kelland for £5,350 and it was a term of the agreement that £3,000 should remain on mortgage. Conveyance of the premises took place in September 1904 with the creation of a legal mortgage in favour of the Kellands for £3,000 on 27 January 1905.

Mr Justice Eve held that it was immaterial whether, at the time when that mortgage was created, the mortgagees had notice of the debentures of 1901.

'Any equity which attached to the property contracted to be purchased was, throughout, subject to the paramount equity of the unpaid vendors. The legal mortgage which secures the unpaid purchase-moneys must, in my opinion, take priority over any charge... to persons claiming through the company.'

He made an order against the company and their debenture holders for foreclosure.

It is noteworthy that in that case the debenture concerned had been properly registered under section 14 of the Companies Act, 1900, which was in similar terms to section 95 of the Companies Act, 1948. The mortgage which took priority to it had not been registered.

The principle appears to be that an unpaid seller who has parted with the legal title has a lien on the property, whether it is real estate or a chattel. This right in respect of goods is expressly preserved by the Sale of Goods Act 1979, section 39 (1) (a), 'Notwithstanding that the property in the goods has passed to the buyer', the unpaid seller can exercise his lien so long as the goods are in his possession. If he relinquishes possession in exchange for a promise of an equitable charge over the goods, that equitable charge takes priority over any other equitable charge, even if created earlier and registered. This is because the company has in fact only acquired the 'equity of redemption': that is, the right to acquire beneficial ownership on the paying off of the charge. Debenture holders and their receiver can never be in a better position than the company and therefore they are subject to such a charge.

That is made abundantly clear from in *re Connolly Brothers Ltd (No.2)* (1912). The company had debentures, issued in 1901 and, again, registered under the Companies Act, 1900, which created a floating charge on their whole undertaking and all property present and future. One of the conditions of the debenture was that the company should not be at liberty to create any mortgage or charge in priority to the debentures. In 1904, the company wanted to buy some property in Manchester but had no funds available. The directors therefore asked a Mrs O'Reilly to lend them £1,000 to enable them to purchase it for £1,050, and promised her a charge on the property to secure the sum to be advanced. She agreed and the conveyance took place. The company subsequently gave Mrs O'Reilly's solicitors, who held the title deeds, a memorandum in which it acknowledged that he held the deeds with intent by the company to create an equitable charge on the property and an undertaking to execute a legal mortgage if called upon so to do. This charge was not registered under the Companies Act, or elsewhere.

Later it was claimed that the debentures took priority. Mr Justice Warrington held that Mrs O'Reilly's unregistered charge took priority over the debentures. He said that her case could be put in either of two ways:

'By virtue of the doctrine of subrogation, she stands in the place of the vendor and therefore has the benefit of the vendor's lien. She did not advance this money unconditionally. She agreed to make this advance for the purpose and sole purpose of paying off the purchase money and under a contemporaneous agreement that she was to have a charge on the property.'

The second way of putting it, he found conclusive:

'The debentures, so far as this after-acquired property is concerned, amount to nothing more than a contract by the company to give the debenture holders a security upon that particular item of property ... but only on such interest as the company may in fact acquire....

'The company never acquired ... any interest in this property at all − except subject to an obligation to give Mrs O'Reilly a charge....

'The security acquired by Mrs O'Reilly takes priority over the debentures because it takes priority over the interest of the company itself.... Nothing was subject to the trust deed except what one may describe as the "equity of redemption"...'.

The Court of Appeal unanimously approved this judgment. Lord Cozens-Hardy M.R. said:

'All the company in equity obtained was the equity of redemption in the property, subject to Mrs O'Reilly's charge.'

Lord Justice Buckley said,

'If the company obtained the property, subject to contractual obligation to give a first charge on it to Mrs O'Reilly, then the debenture holders can get no more.'

Once again an unregistered charge prevailed over registered debentures.

The same principle was upheld by the Privy Council, (Lord Cross of Chelsea, Lord Simon of Glaisdale and Lord Edmund-Davies) in *Security Trust Co.* v. *The Royal Bank of Canada* (1976).

The facts are more complex but the judicial committee unanimously approved the decision in *re Connolly Brothers Ltd,* and for the same reasons. Once again an unregistered mortgage was given priority over a registered debenture.

That being so, one may well wonder why effect was not given to this doctrine in *re Bond Worth Ltd.* In that case, legal title in the goods was transferred to the buyers only on the condition that they hold the title subject beneficial ownership of the unpaid sellers. Mr Justice Slade held that this amounted to a charge by way of security, but he went on to hold that it was void against the receiver for the debenture holders because it was not registered under section 95 of the Companies Act, 1948.

His explanation for not applying the principle of *re Connolly Brothers Ltd* is contained in these words:

'Though this argument has some superficial attraction, I do not think that the *Connolly* decision, when properly analysed, is of any assistance to Monsanto.

'As will have appeared, that was a case where A, the purchaser of the relevant property from B, had, before completion, entered into a contract for good consideration, to grant a charge over the property in favour of C. Accordingly, the very moment that A acquired the legal estate in the property, A held it in trust to give effect in equity to C's rights, by virtue of the pre-existing contract between A and C.

'In the face of this contract, it could not therefore have been successfully claimed that the purchaser A, even for a moment, acquired more than an equity of redemption in the property, (though it may be observed that the relevant charge, even in that case, was undeniably created by A, rather than the vendor B).

'The case did not even touch the question whether it would have been conceptually possible for the vendor B to except to himself a mortgage in such a manner that the subject matter of the sale, as between A and B, was a mere equity of redemption, so that the transaction involved no express or implied grant back by A in favour of B.

'Notwithstanding the arrangements made between A and C, the transaction as between A and B in the *Connolly* case remains throughout one for the sale of the entire legal and beneficial interest in the property.'

With respect to his lordship, it is difficult to follow his argument. He conceded throughout that the legal and equitable position regarding the sale of goods was no different from that of real property, and he held on his interpretation of the contract that both legal and equitable title had passed to the buyer. The rights of Mrs O'Reilly were second-hand rights in that she was subrogated to, or in ordinary language, stood in the shoes of, the original unpaid vendor.

It is instructive therefore to revert to the case which is the closest analogy to that before him, namely, *Wilson* v. *Kelland,* to which his lordship was referred but which he did not discuss in his judgment.

In *Wilson* v. *Kelland,* a vendor relinquished his lien as unpaid seller over property he had agreed to sell for £5,350 in return for £2,350 and a contractual promise that he would be granted an equitable charge over the property of £3,000. The charge which was subsequently created was unregistered but was held to prevail over an earlier created and registered floating charge over all assets, present or future of the company. The reason being that the company has only acquired an equity of redemption for the property.

In *re Bond Worth Ltd,* a vendor relinquished his lien as unpaid seller over property he had agreed to sell for over £500,000 in return for a contractual promise that he would remain beneficial owner of the goods: which his lordship held to be an equitable charge, created by the purchaser in favour of the vendor, for the whole of the purchase price.

Why then, vis-à-vis the debenture holders and their receiver who had no greater rights than the company itself, were they not deferred to the equitable rights of the unpaid seller?

The argument from the *Connolly* decision is not merely superficially attractive but entirely logical and convincing.

The legal position can be stated in simple propositions.

Proposition 1: A seller who has agreed to sell real or personal property to a buyer has a lien (a right) to retain the property until he is paid in full by the buyer, even though the ownership of the property has by contract, under English law, passed to the buyer.

Proposition 2: If, in reliance on the contractual promise of a company (the buyer), that it will enter into an obligation to pay the full agreed price and will, until payment, grant to the unpaid seller an equitable charge on the property, the unpaid seller relinquishes his lien on the goods, the company will acquire the legal title to the property solely subject to the rights of the unpaid seller. These rights must, as a matter of law and equity, prevail over any debenture, whatever its terms, registered before the transaction for the simple reason that all the company has acquired is merely the right to acquire beneficial ownership to accompany its legal ownership, on payment of the full purchase price.

Proposition 3: The debenture holders, and their receiver, can never attain greater rights than the company itself has. If the company has acquired by contract only the legal title to goods, subject to the real ownership being in the unpaid seller, the receiver has no greater rights.

Proposition 4: In all this, it is irrelevant whether or not the equity of the real owner is registered or not. If a company buys only the shell of a crab, the debenture holders through the receiver, cannot claim its contents. The rights of the debenture holders attach only to the shell.

Therefore, if a company acquires the legal title to goods subject to an equitable charge for the whole of the purchase price, a receiver appointed by the debenture holders can never acquire more than the company had: in short, nothing more than the equity of redemption, i.e. the right to become owner in law and in equity by paying the unpaid seller in full for the goods.

This, however, is not what Mr Justice Slade decided in *re Bond Worth Ltd.* He held that the unpaid seller's equitable interest in the goods and their proceeds constituted a floating charge which must have been properly registered under section 95 of the Companies Act, 1948, if it were to prevail against a receiver appointed on behalf of earlier debenture holders.

Apart from this, it is difficult to understand how he could conclude that an express term of a contract which reserved equitable and beneficial ownership to the unpaid seller could be effective to pass both legal title equitable *and* beneficial ownership to the buyers. He said,

'the proper manner of construing the retention of title clause, together with all the other relevant provisions of the contract of sale read as a whole, is to regard them as effecting a sale in which the *entire* property in the Acrilan passed to Bond Worth.' (Author's italics.)

He treated the contract thereafter as 'a security, *eo instanti* given back by Bond Worth to the vendor, Monsanto.'

But even if he were right about this, the equitable charge, given *eo instanti* as he put it, appears indistinguishable from that given *eo instanti* in *Wilson* v. *Kelland,* in *re Connolly* and *Security Trust Co.* v. *The Royal Bank of Canada.* Bond Worth had only acquired an equity of redemption and nothing more and therefore the debenture holders' rights only attached to that.

It is submitted therefore that even if it were to amount only to an equitable charge, such a retention to title clause does not require registration under any part of section 95 of the Companies Act, 1948.

6.11   Personal liability of a receiver

In circumstances where a company re-sells goods subject to a retention of title clause without the express or implied authority of the owners, the owners may claim damages for conversion of the goods, which damages will be quantified in accordance with the principles set out in the Tort (Interference with Goods) Act 1977. In essence, the damages will normally be not the price at which the seller would be prepared to sell to the intending buyer but the damages suffered by the wrongful disposal.

In the event of a liquidation of a company, such damages will, when quantified by a court, rank only with the claims of unsecured creditors and after those of the priority and secured creditors such as debenture holders. Moreover claims for damages for a tort, as distinct from claims for damages for breach of contract, are excluded from proof in a liquidation, until quantified by judgment (Companies Act, 1948, section 317).

But in the event of an unauthorised sale by a receiver, he will be personally liable to the owner for the damages.

Two situations may arise: where the receiver sells the goods without knowing of the retention of title clause, and where he knows of the retention clause. In the first case, he will be personally liable for damages for conversion, but will be entitled to an indemnity out of the company's assets in priority to the claims of the debenture holders: *Scott* v. *Nesbitt* (1808); *re Rylands Glass Co.* (1905).

Where the receiver knows of the retention of title clause and yet sells the goods, it would appear that he will be liable for damages for conversion without right of recourse to the funds of the company. It is immaterial that he thinks the retention clause is not valid, even if he has cause.

This will apply even where he purports to vest the property of the goods in a 'hive-down' company. The goods are not the property of the parent company to which the receiver has been appointed. The proceedings for damages should be launched against the receiver personally and not against the company in receivership since it is not a tort by the company; and even if damages were recovered against the company, they would only rank after judgment with unsecured creditors and are therefore likely to be irrecoverable in the usual circumstances of a liquidation.

If the receiver has paid to the debenture holders the proceeds of the sale of goods which were not the company's to sell, he may well not be able to recover from them such monies, because these are monies paid under a mistake of law rather than fact. But in any event, the damages and costs for which he will have to become liable will inevitably exceed the price at which he has sold off the goods.

However, whether the unauthorised sale is by the company or its receiver, the vendor with a retention clause will also be able to claim that the company is bailee of the goods and therefore in a fiduciary position. Thereby, he can hold the company or the receiver liable to account for the value of the goods under the tracing principles set out in *re Hallett's Estate* (1880), and exemplified in the *Romalpa* case itself. If the proceeds of sale can be traced into the company on the receiver's account, the full amount can be recovered. If the price has not been paid by the sub-purchaser, the unpaid vendor can recover it directly from him.

6.12   The position of a liquidator

The appointment of a receiver by debenture holders does not by any means necessarily result in the company being wound up. If a company is wound up compulsorily, for any of the reasons specified in the Companies Act, 1948, the operative date from which the winding up is deemed to commence is the date of the petition: section 229 (2). That does not mean that the presentation of a petition necessarily means that a company will be wound up. The petition may well be dismissed. It only means that if a winding-up order is made by the court it relates back to the date on which the petition was presented. This may have the effect of invalidating transactions which have taken place subsequent to the presentation of the petition.

In the case of a voluntary liquidation, the operative date from which it is deemed to have taken place is the date of the resolution of the company to wind up, even where the company is later liquidated under the supervision of the court.

The effect of a winding-up order by the court is to deprive the directors of all authority over the company's affairs and to terminate the contracts of all employees or agents. The passing of a voluntary resolution to wind up apparently does not have the same effect: Companies Act, 1948, sections 285 (2) and 296 (2); *Deaway Trading Ltd* v. *Calverley* (1973).

Once a liquidator has been appointed, the assets of the company become available to him to satisfy the company's debts and liabilities. But, unlike a trustee in bankruptcy, the company's assets do not vest in him personally. He is only the company's agent. The Companies Act merely confers powers on him equivalent to those of the directors. If he executes documents or brings actions or defends them, he must do so in the name of the company: Companies Act, 1948, section 245 (1) (1) and (2) (b). He, therefore, has no personal title to the company's assets and it must follow that his position is no better so far as goods in the possession of the company are concerned than that of a receiver appointed by debenture holders.

It is true that the court does have power to vest any of the company's assets in the liquidator under the Companies Act, 1948, section 244, but this is rarely done.

The company remains the legal owner of its assets but ceases to be beneficial owner of them from the date on which the winding-up is deemed to commence: *Ayerst* v. *C & K (Construction) Ltd* (1976).

The only assets, therefore, which the liquidator has the power to sell to satisfy the company's liabilities are those which the company owned at the commencement of the winding-up.

6.13 Registration of charges

The Companies Act, 1948, requires that certain charges, specified in section 95 (2) shall be recorded in its registered office and filed with the Registrar of Companies.

The effect of non-registration is set out in section 95 (1):

'... every charge created ... by a company registered in England and being a charge to which this section applies shall, so far as any security on the company's property or undertaking is conferred thereby, be void against the liquidator and any creditor of the company, unless the prescribed particulars of the charge, together with the instrument, if any, by which the charge is created or evidenced, are delivered to or received by the registrar of companies for registration in the manner required by this Act within 21 days after the date of its creation.'

Three descriptions of charges may be relevant. These are:

95 (2) (c): '... a charge created or evidenced by an instrument which, if executed by an individual, would require registration as a Bill of Sale.'

95 (2) (e): 'a charge on book debts of the company.'

95 (2) (f): 'a floating charge on the undertaking or property of the company.'

So far as the first category is concerned, it will be observed that the Bills of Sale Act, 1878, and the Amendment Act, 1882, only cover the instrument whereby an individual (not a company), sells goods to another without parting with possession. Moreover, documents are not bills of sale if they are merely 'transfers of goods in the ordinary course of business of any trade ... or documents in the ordinary course of business as proof of the possession or control of goods': Bills of Sale Act, 1878, section 4; *re Hamilton Young & Co.* (1905).

Book debts are debts due to the company which arise out of its ordinary trading transactions, but it has been held that a charge on such debts only requires registration if the book debt is in existence at the time the charge is created: *Paul & Frank Ltd* v. *Discount Bank (Overseas) Ltd* (1966). It does not therefore apply to contractual obligations regarding future book debts.

The retention of title clause in *Romalpa* was not a charge over a book debt because no charge was created over assets belonging to the company, since both the goods and the proceeds of sale throughout the transaction belonged to the original seller. The Irish case which holds to the contrary, *re Interview Ltd* (1975), is not correct and the point was never argued before the court. A charge is subject to this provision only where the chose in action, the book debt, exists as the property of the company at the time when a charge over it is created.

The expression 'a floating charge on the undertaking or property of the company' is highly ambiguous, and it is a matter of debate whether what was intended is a charge over the whole property of the company, or whether it is sufficient if the charge extends only to part of the undertaking and part of the property. In *Mercantile Bank of India Ltd* v. *Chartered Bank of India Australia and China* (1938), it was held that a floating charge over the whole undertaking was meant, but a floating charge over part only of a company's property was caught by the section. It therefore was held in that case that a floating charge over the company's goods was registrable. Mr Justice Slade in *re Bond Worth Ltd,* having held that what was created by the retention clause in that case was no more than the creation of a 'floating equitable charge over four categories of charged assets' for the purpose of securing payment of the purchase prices, held that these were caught by this provision of section 95. But it has no application if neither the goods nor the proceeds thereof are the property of the company.

6.14　What is registrable under section 95?

It will be noted that under section 95 only charges 'created' by a company are registrable. In the High Court in the *Romalpa* case, it was argued that the tracing claims were in effect charges on book debts for the purpose of section 95 (1) (2) (e) of the Companies Act. Mr Justice Mocatta dismissed his argument with the words

'If property in the foil never passed to the defendants, with the result that the proceeds of sub-sales belonged in equity to the plaintiffs, section 95 (1) had no application.'

The point was not taken in the Court of Appeal.

In *re Bond Worth Ltd* where the sellers had retained the equitable title and purported to allow the legal title to pass to the buyers, Mr Justice Slade held that it was the *buyers* who created thereby an equitable charge over the goods in question. A charge, he held, which required to be registered as a floating charge under section 95 (1) (2) (d).

But charges which come into effect, not as the result of contractual obligations, but as the result of operation of common law or equity are not charges 'created' by companies and do not require registration. Thus, an unpaid vendor's lien or the charge which a judgment creditor acquires when he takes property in execution or anticipated trust receipts do not need to be registered: *Capital Finance Co. Ltd* v. *Stokes* (1969); *London & Cheshire Insurance Co. Ltd* v. *Laplagrene Property Co. Ltd* (1971); *Brunton* v. *Electrical Engineering Corporation* (1892).

Moreover, even if unregistered, a charge created by the company is binding as between the creditor who holds the charge and the company: *Independent Automative Sales Ltd* v. *Knowles & Foster* (1962). It is, by the wording of the statute, invalid *only* against the liquidator or other creditors (section 95 (1)). So that if the charge is realised by the creditor before the company is wound up, that creditor obtains an impregnable title, good against both liquidator and other creditors. Only in the event of liquidation does section 95 come into operation, and nothing done before that can stop the company paying off a secured but unregistered charge or prevent the holder of that charge from enforcing his security: *re Cardiff Workmen's Cottage Co. Ltd* (1906).

The receiver of a company has no greater rights than the company itself and as such is bound by charges that the company has created, even if unregistered: *Parsons* v. *Sovereign Bank of Canada* (1913). This principle appears to have been overlooked by Mr Justice Slade in his judgment in *re Bond Worth Ltd.* He said that unregistered charges were void against 'any creditor of Bond Worth'.

The position of a receiver is therefore fundamentally different from that of a liquidator of a company being wound up so far as unregistered charges are concerned [see also 8.04].

Chapter 7

The Romalpa Case

7.01   Terms of A.I.V.'s retention clause
The preceding chapters have summarised the effect of the decisions
of English courts in cases about retention of title and it is now
proposed to examine these in detail, particularly in the light of
their historical sequence.

The case of *Aluminium Industrie Vaassen B.V.* v. *Romalpa
Aluminium Ltd* came before Mr Justice Mocatta in the Queen's
Bench Division of the High Court on 3 February 1975 and he
delivered a reserved judgment on 11 February of that year.

The retention of title clause with which he was concerned read
in the English version of the Dutch original:

'Clause 13. The ownership of the material to be delivered by A.I.V.
will only be transferred to purchaser when he has met all that is
owing to A.I.V., no matter on what grounds.

'Until the date of payment, purchaser, if A.I.V. so desires, is
required to store this material in such a way that it is clearly the
property of A.I.V.

'A.I.V. and purchaser agree that, if purchaser should make (a)
new object(s) from the material, mixes this material with (an)other
object(s) or if this material in any way whatsoever becomes a
constituent of (an)other object(s), A.I.V. will be given the ownership of this (these) new object(s) as surety [*sic*] of the full payment of what purchaser owes A.I.V.

'To this end A.I.V. and purchaser now agree that the ownership of the article(s) in question, whether finished or not, are to be transferred to A.I.V. and that this transfer of ownership will be considered to have taken place through and at the moment of the single operation or event by which the material is converted into (a) new object(s), or is mixed with or becomes a constituent of (an)other object(s). Until the moment of full payment of what purchaser owes A.I.V., purchaser shall keep the object(s) in question for A.I.V. in his capacity of fiduciary owner and, if required, shall store this (these) object(s) in such a way that it (they) can be recognised as such.

'Nevertheless, purchaser will be entitled to sell these objects to a third party within the framework of the normal carrying on of his business and to deliver them on condition that − if A.I.V. so requires − purchaser, as long as he has not fully discharged his debt to A.I.V. shall hand over to A.I.V. the claims he has against his buyer emanating from this transaction.'

It will be seen that this in essence falls into three parts: a simple retention of title clause, a current account clause, and an aggregation clause.

7.02 The issues in the High Court

A.I.V. supplied aluminium foil to Romalpa Ltd until 1 November 1974 when the latter's banker, Hume Corporation Ltd, appointed a receiver pursuant to powers contained in a debenture. The day before the appointment of the receiver, A.I.V. issued a writ against Romalpa and the same day obtained from Mr Justice Cusack an interlocutory injunction restraining the company from disposing of aluminium foil in their possession.

By their statement of claim, A.I.V. sought, *inter alia,*

(i)   a declaration that they were entitled to a charge on the sum of £35,152.66 held in an account by the receiver, representing the proceeds of the sale of aluminium foil supplied by A.I.V. to Romalpa.

(ii) a declaration that aluminium foil to the value of £50,235 held by the receiver originating in deliveries to Romalpa by A.I.V. was the latter's foil; and an order for delivery up.

(iii) alternatively, and as the judge put it, 'very much as a third string to their claim', judgment for the price.

The receiver admitted holding foil to the value of £50,235 which were deliveries by A.I.V. to Romalpa. In the proceedings, he conceded that A.I.V. were the owners of this unsold foil and were entitled to an order for its delivery up. He thereby agreed that clause 13 was effective to retain the ownership of the foil which actually came into his possession on assuming his office.

The case therefore concerned solely the sum of £35,152.66 the proceeds of sale of foil to various third parties, which sum the receiver had placed in a separate account. He did not dispute that at the date of his appointment Romalpa owed A.I.V. £122,230.

So far as the £35,152.66 was concerned the judge said:

'It is common ground that the effect of the clause is that, whilst money was owing by the defendants to the plaintiffs, any aluminium foil delivered by the plaintiffs to the defendants, whilst still in their possession, was held by them as bailees.'

It is clear therefore that counsel for Romalpa had conceded that, under the clause, the status of Romalpa was that of the bailee of the property of A.I.V.

In spite of the wording of this last paragraph of clause 13, both counsel were agreed that there was no express authority to sell on unmixed foil and that a term had to be implied into the contract that Romalpa were entitled to do so.

It was argued on behalf of the receiver that once the foil was sold on, the relationship between A.I.V. and Romalpa became purely that of debtor and creditor – with the result that A.I.V. were merely unsecured creditors in the impending insolvency.

Against this, the plaintiffs argued that because the defendants were bailees, it inevitably followed that a fiduciary relationship existed between the parties. The judge explained:

'It was not necessary, said the plaintiffs, to find as a prerequisite of the right to trace an express or constructive trust. The equitable proprietary remedy followed as a consequence of the finding that the defendants were bailees.'

A fiduciary relationship is one between two persons where one is under an obligation to use rights and powers in the interest of the other. The relationship of trustee and beneficiary is one such fiduciary relationship, but equity does not require a full formal trust before holding that one person is under a duty to account to the other. It followed that because there was that relationship of bailor and bailee, there was a duty to account to A.I.V. Therefore, equity gave a right to the receipts.

Everything, therefore, flowed from the admission by Romalpa's counsel that the defendants were bailees of A.I.V.'s goods. Since they were bailees of another's goods, they were in a fiduciary position; since they were in a fiduciary position they were in equity obligated to account to A.I.V. for all the proceeds of the sale of their goods.

The judgment in *re Hallett's Estate* (1880) was quoted in support of the last limb of that proposition. In it, Lord Jessel M.R. said:

'The modern doctrine of equity as regards property disposed of by persons in a fiduciary position is a very clear and well-established doctrine. You can, if the sale were rightful, take the proceeds of the sale, if you can identify them.'

In another passage, he made it clear that in this principle there was no distinction between formal trustees and other persons in a fiduciary position.

'Has it ever been suggested, until very recently, that there was any distinction between an express trustee, or an agent, or a bailee, or a collector of rents or anybody else in a fiduciary position. I have never heard, until quite recently, such a distinction suggested.... It can have no foundation in principle, because the beneficial ownership is the same, wherever the legal ownership may be.'

Later, Lord Jessel M.R. dealt expressly with the position of bailees.

'Now that being the established doctrine of equity on this point, I will take the case of the pure bailee. If the bailee sells the goods bailed, the bailor can in equity follow the proceeds.... Therefore there is no difficulty in following the rule of equity and deciding that in a case of mere bailee ... you can follow the money.'

Mr Justice Mocatta therefore held that clause 13 created a fiduciary relationship and not just a simple debtor/creditor relationship and therefore, the plaintiffs were entitled to the relief they sought.

7.03 Did the retention of title clause create a charge on the company's book debts?

He also dealt with another point in the words:

'A further point made by counsel for the defendants was that if the plaintiffs were to succeed in their tracing claim this would, in effect, be a method available against a liquidator to a creditor of avoiding the provisions establishing the need to register charges on book debts: see section 95 (1) (2) (e) of the Companies Act, 1948.

He used this only as an argument against the effect of clause 13 contended for by counsel for the plaintiffs. As to this, I think counsel for the plaintiffs' answer was well founded, namely that if property in the foil never passed to the defendants, with the result that the proceeds of sub-sales belonged in equity to the plaintiffs, section 95 (1) had no application.'

Section 95 (1) of the Companies Act, 1948, is set out in [6.13]. This point was to be raised in later cases and has been discussed in [6.13].

7.04 *Romalpa* in the Court of Appeal

In the Court of Appeal, counsel for Romalpa was allowed to amend his notice of appeal to raise other issues. Judgment was given on 16 January 1976.

It there appeared that the sales to sub-purchasers had been made by the receiver and that he had kept those receipts separate from others. Said Lord Justice Roskill,

'There was no suggestion that the sub-sales were other than authorised by the plaintiffs or that the sub-purchasers concerned did not acquire a valid title to the several quantities of foil.'

This represented two further substantial concessions by counsel for Romalpa, and they pose questions which have been discussed already, namely: Has a receiver any power to sell goods which he knows are still the property of the vendor [6.11]? Does a sub-purchaser get a good title under section 25 (2) of the Sale of Goods Act, 1893 (or section 25 (1) of the Sale of Goods Act 1979), if he knows the title is still vested in the original seller [4.11]?

Since these questions were not raised, Lord Justice Roskill correctly, it is submitted with respect, held that the only question before the Court of Appeal was

'whether there was a fiduciary relationship between the plaintiffs and the defendants which entitles the plaintiffs successfully to claim these monies.'

Unlike Mr Justice Mocatta, he did not base his answer to this question on the concession by counsel that Romalpa were bailees of the goods but upon his construction of the terms of clause 13.

Discussing the contention that the contract simply resulted in the normal relationship of creditor/debtor, he said,

'Clause 13 plainly provides otherwise.

'The plaintiffs as sellers were to retain the property in the goods until all — and I underline *'all'* — that was owing to them had been paid....

'It is obvious that the business purpose of the whole of this clause, read in its context in these general conditions, was to secure the plaintiffs, so far as possible, against the risks of non-payment after they had parted with possession of the goods delivered, whether or not those goods retained their identity after delivery ....

'In the case of unmanufactured goods, this was to be achieved by the plaintiffs retaining the property until all payments due had been made ....

'The burden of counsel for the plaintiff's argument was, first, that all goods dealt with in pursuance of clause 13 were, until *all* debts were discharged, the plaintiffs' goods which the defendants were authorised to sell on the plaintiffs' behalf and for the plaintiffs' account but only within the framework of clause 13. Since the goods were the plaintiffs', the defendants remained accountable to the plaintiffs for them or for their proceeds of sale, so long as any indebtedness whatever remained outstanding from the defendants to the plaintiffs. Hence the creation of the fiduciary relationship on which counsel for the plaintiffs sought to rely.'

Lord Justice Roskill then dealt with the fact that the first part of clause 13 did not authorise Romalpa to sell-on unprocessed the goods which were the property of A.I.V., nor did it prescribe what was to happen to the proceeds of sale if such goods were sold.

'It was common ground at the trial and during argument in this court that some implication had to be made into the first part of clause 13; since, otherwise, the defendants could not lawfully sell the manufactured goods in their possession, at least until they were paid for − for, as already pointed out, they were the plaintiffs' and not the defendants' goods.

'To hold otherwise, as I think both parties accepted, would be to stultify the whole business purpose of these transactions.

'What, if any, implication is to be made beyond that?

'The first part of clause 13 is silent not only as to the power of sale but as to the dealing with any proceeds of the goods lawfully so sold by the defendants.

'Is the admitted power of sale ... fettered or unfettered? If it is fettered, is the fetter that, so long as any indebtedness remained outstanding in any respect from the defendants to the plaintiffs, the defendants after a sub-sale remained accountable to the plaintiffs for all proceeds of sub-sales, not even, as counsel for the defendants pointed out in argument, being able to retain for themselves the profit on any such sales?'

In addition to clause 13, hitherto mentioned, the contract contained two other clauses which Lord Justice Roskill considered of importance.

Clause 25: 'Should purchaser remain in default of any payment for which he is liable to A.I.V. then A.I.V. is entitled to stop all deliveries, irrespective of which contract with purchaser they spring from, and to rescind the contract in question without judicial intervention, all this without prejudicing their right to full compensation and without prejudicing their right to take back at once from purchaser the material by virtue of what is laid down under 13 is still their property.'

Clause 22: 'Payment has to be made nett cash by purchaser not later than fourteen days after the date of invoice, preferably by payment by transfer to the postal giro or banking account of A.I.V. If required a bill of exchange can be drawn. The place of payment for all deliveries is Vaassen (Gld.). This also holds good when a bill is returned unpaid. In spite of any complaints about flaws in the material delivered, purchaser is obliged to pay the purchase price at the time laid down.'

This had been varied subsequently to allow 75 days' credit.

Counsel for Romalpa relied upon that latter clause. As Lord Justice Roskill said:

'Counsel for the defendants relied much on the 75 days' credit, though, as I have already ventured to point out, the problem is the same whatever the length of the credit.

'But the longer the period it can be fairly said the greater the business, if not the legal, force of this part of counsel's argument.

'If the plaintiffs were right, counsel for the defendants argued, then whenever sub-purchasers paid the defendants before the 75 days' credit had expired, the defendants could not use those proceeds in their business for any purpose whatever save for paying their creditors, the plaintiffs; they must always retain those specifically for the plaintiffs' account and pay them over to the plaintiffs unless and until the entirety of outstanding indebtedness was discharged.

'This, he said, would deprive the defendants of all day-to-day finance and, so far from according with business efficacy, would produce precisely the opposite result, for it would cause acute cash-flow problems, and make conduct of the defendants' business impossible.

'This is a formidable argument if one looks at the matter solely from the point of view of the defendants. But this matter has to be regarded in the light of the contractual provisions agreed on by both parties, and the question of business efficacy, in relation to which there are here obvious competing business considerations, must be answered in the light of what both parties expressly agreed on and therefore must be taken also impliedly to have agreed on, and not unilaterally from the point of view of one party only.'

He then concluded that there was, as both counsel agreed, an implied power of sale, and that

'one must imply into the first part of the clause not only the power to sell but also the obligation to account in accordance with the normal fiduciary relationship of principal and agent, bailor and bailee.

'Accordingly ... I find no difficulty in holding that the principles in *re Hallett's Estate* ... are of immediate application and I think the plaintiffs are entitled to trace these proceeds of sale and recover them.'

With that Lord Justice Goff agreed, expressing the view that it was 'a short question of construction.'
He concluded:

'The power of sale to be implied where none has been expressed must be qualified so as not to defeat the intention clearly shown by clause 13 as a whole, including the latter part, which only emphasises this.... The implied power must therefore ... be a power to sell, not for the defendants' own account but for the account of the plaintiffs', unless and until all monies owing be paid.'

Lord Justice Megaw also thought that the question was one of the true construction of clause 13: 'a short one though ... but by no means an easy one.'
His conclusion was:

'The power of sale to be implied in the first part of clause 13, where none had been expressed, must be such as not to defeat the intention shown by clause. It is not a power to sell for the defendants' own account but it is a power to sell for the account of the plaintiffs.'

7.05   The aggregation clause in *Romalpa*

As will be seen the *ratio decidendi* of the case in the Court of Appeal lay in four propositions.

(1)   The simple retention of title clause in the first part of clause 13 validly retained the property of the goods to A.I.V.

(2)   Since there was no express power to sell-on processed or admixed goods made with the goil, a power for Romalpa to sell-on the foil itself had to be implied to give commercial effectiveness to the clause, under the *Moorcock* doctrine.

(3)   Under the same doctrine, a term had likewise to be implied, similar to that in the last paragraph of clause 13, that Romalpa were to hold the whole of the proceeds of sale for the benefit of A.I.V.

(4)   Hence A.I.V. were entitled to the proceeds of sale in the receiver's hands.

The case is therefore authority for the proposition that simple retention of title clauses, current account clauses and proceeds of sale clauses are all valid in English law.

The validity of the aggregation clause in the second part of clause 13 was not directly considered except as confirmatory evidence of an overall intention to reserve the title to A.I.V. until payment. Observations about it must therefore be regarded as *obiter dicta,* but it is interesting to see the views taken of such clauses by three judges in the Court of Appeal.

Lord Justice Roskill said:

'In the case of mixed or manufactured goods, more elaborate provisions were made and indeed were obviously required if the avowed objects of clause 13 were to be achieved in the case of the latter class of goods.

'The plaintiffs were to be given the ownership of these mixed or manufactured goods as "surety" for "full payment". "Surety" I think in this context must mean, as counsel for the plaintiffs contended, "security".

'This is as between the defendants and the plaintiffs, and it is not necessary to consider how far these provisions would protect the plaintiffs against adverse claims, at any rate in this country, by third parties.

'Further the clause later provides that until "full payment" is made the defendants shall keep the mixed goods for the plaintiffs as "fiduciary owners" — not perhaps the happiest of phrases, but one which suggests, at least to an English lawyer, that in relation to mixed or manufactured goods there was produced what in English law would be called a fiduciary relationship in this respect.

'The clause goes on to give to the defendants an express power of sale of such goods, and the right to deliver them; and adds an obligation on the defendants, if required by the plaintiffs to do so, to assign (to use English legal language) to the plaintiffs the benefit of any claim against a sub-purchaser so long as the defendants have not fully discharged all their indebtedness to the plaintiffs.

'For my part, I accept that this last-mentioned provision is not itself an equitable assignment in English law. But I think that counsel for the plaintiffs is right in his general approach to the construction of the second part of clause 13.

'Like the first part, it contemplates the re-sale by the defendants of goods which at the time of such re-sale were to be the property of the plaintiffs and not of the defendants.

'The second part of clause 13 clearly contemplates the creation of a fiduciary relationship in relation to mixed goods; and the assignment provisions are, as I think, clearly designed to give the plaintiffs, if they so require, an additional security to recover debts otherwise payable to the defendants but not paid to them by the sub-purchasers, if the defendants have failed to discharge all or any of their current indebtedness to the plaintiffs.'

From that it would appear that his lordship accepted that A.I.V. could become the owners of admixed goods, that the defendants could validly enter into an obligation to hold the proceeds of such admixed goods for the account of A.I.V. and that this obligation created a fiduciary relationship which enabled them to trace the proceeds of sales of admixed goods. But these matters were, of course, not fully argued before his lordship.

In relation to the aggregation part of clause 13, Lord Justice Goff made reference to arguments which are not otherwise mentioned in the judgments.

'The argument is that under that clause there is no equitable assignment of the book debts until the plaintiff requires the defendants ... "to hand over to A.I.V. the claims he has against the buyer". Further, that as no such requirement was made before the security crystallised by the appointment of the receiver, any equitable assignment resulting therefrom could only be subject to the security created by the debentures.

'I accept that as far as it goes, but it still leaves the question whether one should then·construe the power as entitling the defendants to sell and use the proceeds as and when received for their own benefit unless and until required to assign the debt, or whether ... it is implicit that the proceeds of sale when received on their account and the right to call for an assignment is ancillary only.'

Lord Justice Megaw did not discuss the aggregation clause.

7.06   Criticism of the *Romalpa* judgment

Less than two years later, in the *re Bond Worth* case, which will be examined later, Mr Justice Slade commented on the Court of Appeal judgment in *Romalpa*. On reading these comments it becomes apparent that he was less than happy with it as authority, even though he was bound by it, and he managed to distinguish it from the case before him. (The quotations are from the full transcript of Mr Justice Slade's judgment, as delivered and not from the versions which appear in the law reports.)

Mr Justice Slade said:

'All three judgments seem to have accepted that there was no conceptual difficulty in the proposition that, as between itself and its sub-purchasers, the defendant sold as principal, but that as between itself and the plaintiffs, those goods which it was selling within its implied authority from the plaintiffs were the plaintiffs' goods, which it was selling as agent for the plaintiffs, to whom it remained fully accountable. Roskill L.J. expressly said so:

"If an agent lawfully sells his principal's goods, he stands in a fiduciary relationship to his principal and remains account-able to his principal for those goods and their proceeds. 'A bailee is in like position in relation to his bailor's goods. What,

then, is there here to relieve the defendants from their obligations to account to the plaintiffs for those goods of the plaintiffs which they lawfully sell to sub-purchasers? The fact that
they so sold them as principals does not, as I think, affect
their relationship with the plaintiffs; nor (as at present ad-
vised) do I think ... that the sub-purchasers could on this
analysis have sued the plaintiffs upon the sub-contracts as
undisclosed principals for, say, breach of warranty of quality."

'The facts of the *Romalpa* case have this much in common
with those of the present case: In each instance the relevant
clause, by necessary implication, left the purchaser at liberty
both to sell the relevant goods and to use them unrestrictedly
for the purposes of manufacture, at least in the ordinary course
of business. For the purpose of my present decision therefore, it
is perhaps unfortunate that the decisions in *ex parte White,
Foley* v. *Hill* and *Randell's* case do not appear to have been
cited in argument before either court in the *Romalpa* case. If
they had been cited, the judgments of those courts would no
doubt have explained specifically why the principles exemplified
in these three' earlier decisions presented no obstacle to the
crucial conclusion that at all material times, up to and including
sale, a presently subsisting fiduciary relationship existed between vendor and purchaser in regard to the goods or their
proceeds.'

Mr Justice Slade therefore made two criticisms of the judgments
in the Court of Appeal.

The first was that there were 'conceptional' difficulties in the
proposition that Romalpa could sell-on both as agents for A.I.V.
and as principals on their own account. With respect, what he
found difficulty with is a well-recognised principle of English
commercial law, and exemplified in numerous cases about com-
modities and stock-jobbers. It is submitted, with respect, that the
sentence of Lord Roskill (as he now is) summarises the position
accurately.

Mr Justice Slade's second criticism was that he found the judgment inconsistent with the cases he mentions which were not
cited in the Court of Appeal.

The force of this criticism of the *Romalpa* decision is directed to the view that, on the facts, Romalpa were not in a fiduciary position.

It is therefore proposed to examine these three cases in detail in order to consider whether there is in them anything inconsistent with the Court of Appeal's decision in *Romalpa.*

In *ex parte White* (1873) cotton goods were sent by Towle & Co. to one Nevill on terms that he sold them on such terms as he pleased and did not pay for them until he had in fact disposed of them. The question whether Nevill was in a fiduciary relationship with Towle, or whether it was a simple creditor/debtor relationship, was disposed of by Lord Justice James with the words:

'It does not appear that he was ever expected to return any particular contract, or the names of the persons with whom he had dealt.

'He pursued his own course in dealing with the goods, and frequently before sale he manipulated them to a very considerable extent by pressing, dyeing and otherwise altering their character, changing them as much as wheat would be changed by being turned into flour; and he sold them on what terms he pleased as to price and length of credit.

'No question appears ever to have been raised as to whether he was entitled to do this; we must take it that he did not commit any breach of duty in so doing.

'That is quite inconsistent with the notion that he was acting in a fiduciary character in respect of those goods.

'If he was entitled to alter them, to manipulate them, to sell them at any price that he thought fit after they had been so manipulated, and was still only liable to pay for them at a price fixed beforehand, without any reference to the price at which he had sold them, or to anything else than the fact of his having sold them in a certain month, it seems to me impossible to say that the produce of the goods so sold was the money of the consignors or that the relation of vendor and purchaser existed between Towle & Co. and the different persons to whom he sold the goods.'

Mr Justice Slade apparently saw some analogy between the facts in that case and those in *Romalpa*. But in *ex parte White* case property in the goods clearly passed to Nevill and the only difference from the usual agreement to sell was the terms on which he was allowed to pay for them. It would not appear to be relevant to a situation where title was expressly retained in the vendor.

The House of Lords' case of *Foley* v. *Hill* was the one in which it was held that the relationship between banker and customer was that between debtor and creditor. Money is not by definition goods. *South Australian Insurance Co.* v. *Randell* turned on whether a miller who received farmers' corn for grinding but was under no obligation to return the very same corn had an insurable interest in the corn.

It is difficult to see what assistance any of these cases would have been to the Court of Appeal in its task of construing clause 13 of the Romalpa agreement. *Randell's* case does however raise points about the nature of bailment and might suggest doubts as to whether counsel's concession that Romalpa were bailees of A.I.V.'s goods was correct in law. As we have seen, the Court of Appeal judgments were not based on that concession, but it is submitted that it was in fact correct.

7.07   The English law of bailment

With respect, Mr Justice Slade's criticism of *Romalpa* appears to be based on two fallacies. His first is that there can be no bailment in English law unless there is an obligation on the bailee to return to the bailor the very thing bailed.

In fact, his lordship expressly approved the argument advanced by counsel that

'it is quite inconsistent with the concept of a trust or fiduciary relationship ... that Bond Worth should be free to use the Acrilan fibre and other categories of assets subject to the retention of title clause for the purpose of its own business and manufacturing processes.'

The three cases mentioned were alleged to support this proposition. In relation to the *South Australian Insurance Co.* v. *Randell* case, he summarised the decision in the words

'The Privy Council rejected the insurers' submission, on the grounds that where there is a delivery of property on a contract for an equivalent in money, or some other valuable commodity, and not for the return of *the identical subject matter in its original form or an altered form,* this is a sale and not a bailment.'

If that is what the Privy Council did indeed decide they were surely in error since not even in 1869, before the Sale of Goods Act, 1893, was a contract of barter or exchange (i.e. for 'some other valuable commodity') a sale of goods. Sale of goods in English law has always required, as section 1 (1) of the Sale of Goods Act, 1893, did, 'a money consideration': *Harrison* v. *Luke* (1845).

Nor does bailment require a return to the bailor of 'the identical subject matter in its original form or altered form'.

The foundation of the modern English law regarding bailment is to be found in a case called *Coggs* v. *Barnard* (or *Bernard*) in the year 1703 and in the judgment in that case of Chief Justice Holt.

The concept of bailment existed from the Middle Ages and the action of detinue lay against a bailee who refused to return a bailor's goods to him. By the middle of the sixteenth century bailment had come to be regarded as essentially contractual in origin.

In addition to that, there was recognised the position of 'the common carrier', a person who 'by his trade' held himself out to carry from one place to another the goods of other people and who by law was responsible for the goods even if they were damaged or lost without fault on his part.

The case of *Coggs* v. *Barnard* did not fit readily into either the contractual or the common-carrier categories. The defendant had promised to collect for a friend various casks of brandy from a wine cellar and deliver them to another. He did so without remuneration and without any express promises as to their safe carriage or delivery, so there could be no *assumpsit* (contract), and he was not a common carrier. On the way to the other wine cellar, some of the casks of brandy fell off the cart and were damaged, and some 180 gallons were lost. The owner sued for his loss.

The case, being thought of great importance, was argued individually by all the judges of the Common Pleas but it is the judgment of Chief Justice Holt which fashioned English law ever since.

He professed to base his judgment on the medieval dissertation *De Legibus et Consuetudinibus Angliae* attributed to the English author known as Bracton and written some time in the reign of Henry III and usually, by guesswork ascribed to around 1250 AD. In truth, Chief Justice Holt seems to have had recourse to Roman law and transcribed it verbatim from Justinian.

He said that there were six forms of bailment and he then went on to detail them as:

(1) *depositum:* goods given by one man to another to keep 'to the use' of the bailor and to return to him in due course or on his directions.

(2) *commodatum:* where goods or chattels are lent for use to a friend gratis, to be returned.

(3) *locatio et conductio:* where goods are left with the bailee for use by him for a consideration called hire.

(4) *vadium:* where goods are delivered in pawn as security for a loan.

(5) where goods are delivered to the bailee to be carried or kept, for the bailee to work on them for a reward.

(6) where goods are delivered to the bailee to be carried or kept for the bailee to work on them without reward.

Two points are worthy of note: the first is that bailment imposes an obligation on the bailee not by reason of contract, agreement or promise but because he has come into possession of the goods of another. In *Coggs* v. *Barnard* the defendant did so voluntarily, but subsequent cases have made it clear that a person can become a bailee voluntarily or involuntarily without it making any alteration to his obligations in law.

Voluntarily or involuntarily is immaterial, except to illustrate the extent of the obligation.

Secondly, the obligation of a bailee is not circumscribed by the obligation to return the chattels bailed to the bailor. It is to conform to the bailor's wishes regarding the disposition of the goods or 'according to his directions'. Bernard would have been no less of a bailee if he had been instructed to deliver the casks of brandy not to another wine cellar but to Gray's Inn for consumption by its members.

This obligation imposed by law clearly extended not merely to the goods themselves but to any product made from them. This is implicit in Sir John Holt's fifth and sixth category and under Roman law there could be a bailment of wine into which grapes had been pressed. This is not merely an obligation to restore the identical object matter in its original form or an altered form, but to hold for the owner whatever resulted from the use of his goods.

Moreover by operation of law, if Tom is allowed by Harry's authority to sub-bail Harry's goods, both have the rights of bailors against sub-bailee. As *Pollock and Wright on Possession* puts it, 'If the bailee of a thing sub-bails it by authority ... both the owner and the first bailee have concurrently the rights of bailor against the third person according to the nature of the sub-bailment'.

In all cases where the bailee, with the consent of the bailor, is allowed to sell-on the bailor's goods, the proceeds are branded with the proprietary rights of the bailor and the bailee holds them as fiduciary for the bailor.

'If the bailee sells the goods bailed, the bailor can in equity follow the proceeds, and can follow the proceeds wherever they can be distinguished, either being actually kept separate, or being mixed up with other moneys.' (Lord Jessel M.R. in *re Hallett*.)

Chapter 8

From Borden to Bond Worth

8.01 The retention clause in the *Borden* case

Judge Rubin Q.C. sitting as a deputy judge of the Chancery Division of the High Court delivered judgment in the case of *Borden (U.K.) Ltd* v. *Scottish Timber Products Ltd* on 15 November 1978.

The retention of title clause read:

'Clause 2: Risk and property

Goods supplied by the Company shall be at the purchaser's risk immediately on delivery to the purchaser or into custody on the purchaser's behalf (whichever is the sooner) and the purchaser should therefore be insured accordingly. Property on the goods supplied hereunder will pass to the customer when

(a) the goods the subject of the contract
(b) all other goods the subject any other contract between the company and the customer which at the time of payment of the full price of the goods sold under the contract, have been delivered to the customer but not paid for in full, have been paid for in full.'

It will be seen that it was, so far as (a) is concerned, a simple retention clause, and so far as (b) is concerned, a current account clause, not for all indebtedness but limited to indebtedness for previous deliveries of goods. The most relevant thing, however, is that there was no aggregation clause [3.05].

The case came before the court on preliminary issues of law. The points of law were formulated in a series of questions but Judge Rubin took the view that the questions did not help in showing the true issues and he formulated his own.

8.02 The agreed facts

Borden (U.K.) Ltd supplied resin to Scottish Timber Products Ltd between 14 February and 16 September 1977, when a receiver was appointed. The resin was delivered by road tanker and stored in tanks which, if full to capacity, held only enough resin to keep the S.T.P. factory working for two days.

When required for use the resin was transferred to a separate tank where it was mixed with wax emulsion and hardeners to form a glue mix. It was then blended with desiccated timber and pressed to form chipboard. Of the final chipboard, the timber components comprised 24% by value and the resin 17%.

8.03 The issues

Judge Rubin held that the following were the issues:

(1)   Did Borden have any proprietary interest at common law in any chipboard manufactured by S.T.P. using the resin supplied by Borden?

(2)   What right, if any, has Borden on the principle of *re Hallett* to trace their resin into its proceeds of sale?

(3)   Whether any such right to trace was a charge which was void by reason of section 95 of the Companies Act, 1948, against creditors of the company.

On the first issue it was Borden's case that it became co-owner of any chipboard manufactured with its resin.

The cases to which the judge was referred all dealt with the accidental admixture of the goods of different parties or the wrongful admixture.

Judge Rubin said:

'The plaintiff has been unable to find any common law authority dealing with a manufacturing process. Perhaps this is not surprising as it cannot have been common for suppliers of raw materials to reserve their title to those materials after delivery to the manufacturer. Unless the terms of the contract of supply contained some special term, I find it difficult to discover any adequate reason why a court in the exercise of a discretion should order the manufacturer of the article to deliver that article to a supplier of a raw material, particularly in a case where the raw material forms only a part and not an outstandingly large part, of the elements required for the manufacturing process.

'For these reasons I am not persuaded that Borden has any common law title to the chipboard for which its resin was used.'

On the second point he said:

'It seemed to me clear from an early stage in the argument that S.T.P. received resin, which remained the property of Borden, as a bailee for Borden, and accordingly a fiduciary relationship was created.

'If, instead of using that resin for manufacture, S.T.P. had re-sold part of it ... on the principle of *in re Hallett's Estate,* Borden would have been able to trace its resin into the proceeds of any such sale.

'That was precisely the conclusion which was reached by the Court of Appeal in *Aluminium Industrie Vaassen B.V.* v. *Romalpa Aluminium Ltd....*

'In the present case, there is no reason even to imply a power to sell resin as resin, let alone a power for S.T.P. to sell it for its own account.

'In the end the defendants' counsel accepted, though with reluctance, that Borden would be entitled to trace into the proceeds of sale any sale of resin as resin.

'The defendants argued that the tracing remedy does not extend where there is a use in manufacture to the manufactured product and its proceeds of sale.

'In my judgment, unless the fiduciary relationship was brought to an end by the use in manufacture, or it is possible to imply a further term into the contract that S.T.P. would be entitled to deal with the chipboard on its own account, there is no reason why the tracing remedy should not extend both to the chipboard and its proceeds of sale.

'Counsel for the defendants argued both strongly and repeatedly that I should imply no terms at all into the contract or if I implied a licence to use the resin in manufacture I should imply no further term.

'This appears to be an argument against his interest, but I agree that there is no scope in the present case for implying any term beyond a bare licence to use in manufacture before payment.

'In *re Hallett's Estate* (13 Ch. D. 696) at p.710, Jessel M.R. after considering the nature of the equitable remedy said:

> "Therefore the moment you establish the fiduciary relationship, the modern rules of equity, as regards following trust money, apply."

and in the last paragraph on that page he said:

> "Now, that being the established doctrine of equity on the point, I will take the case of the pure bailee. If the bailee sells the goods bailed, the bailor can in equity follow the proceeds, and can follow the proceeds wherever they can be distinguished, either being actually kept separate, or being mixed up with other moneys."

'The Master of the Rolls then used an example of a bailee holding a sum of sovereigns which he mixed with his own sovereigns and then invested in a bond or promissory note and said that the only difference was that instead of taking the bond or promissory note, the *cestui que trust* would have a charge for the amount of the trust money on the bond or promissory note.

'If instead of sovereigns, the bailee has some other physical article in his possession which he mixes with his own property in such a way that the trust property could no longer be identified and separated then, in my view, by like reasoning, the *cestui que trust* would have a charge for the value of his property over the mass of the combined property or its proceeds of sale.

'I was referred to *Kirkham* v. *Peel* (1881) as a case which limited the principles of *Hallett's* case. In my judgment that case does no such thing. It merely establishes upon the true construction of the express terms of that contract, assisted by terms to be implied, that the defendants were bound to account for the balance of the proceeds of sale and as they had done this, no question of tracing arose. It is no authority for the proposition that if they had failed to account, the plaintiff would not have been entitled to have a charge upon any asset of the defendants into which he could have traced the proceeds of sale.'

Judge Rubin then discussed the *Romalpa* case and concluded:

'Once it is accepted that initially S.T.P. received resin as a bailee and accordingly that a fiduciary relationship arose, then, in my judgment, the tracing remedies must be available to Borden unless it can be shown that one ought to imply into the contract a power to use the resin in manufacture and if so a liberty in S.T.P. to hold any goods so manufactured to its own account.

'I have already decided that in particular by reason of the limited storage capacity I can imply a licence to use in manufacture but I can see no valid reason why I should imply any further term.

'Indeed, S.T.P.'s counsel urged me very strongly not to imply any terms at all.'

8.04   Did the retention of title clause create a registrable charge?
Judge Rubin then dealt with the final issue:

'The last point is whether the tracing remedy is a charge to which section 95 of the Companies Act, 1948, applies, and is accordingly void for want of registration against the liquidator or any creditor of the company.

'A preliminary point was argued as to whether, since the company is not in liquidation and no creditor is party to the present proceedings, the point could properly be taken by the present defendants.

'It was argued that the second defendant, as a receiver appointed by a creditor, effectively represented the interest of a creditor, for the point to be taken in the present proceedings.

'On the view which I take on the main point it is unnecessary for me to decide the preliminary point.

'Section 95 applies to a charge created by a company. I know that the word "charge" is often used in the context of the equitable remedy which allows a plaintiff to follow his property into a particular asset and have recourse to that asset.

'In my view, it is not a charge in the ordinary sense in which that word is used and is certainly not a charge of the nature envisaged by Section 95. In any event it is difficult to see how the exercise of an equitable remedy by a plaintiff, even if it gives rise to a charge can be said to be a charge created by the company.

'It is interesting to observe that in *Romalpa,* there is no suggestion that the tracing remedy created a registrable charge; indeed in the judgment of Mocatta J., he rejects the argument that if the plaintiff were to succeed in their tracing claim this would, in effect, be a method of avoiding the provision of section 95.'

8.05　Conclusion

Judge Rubin therefore made declarations:

(1)　that Borden had no title at common law in or to any chipboard manufactured with its resin.
(2)　that Borden was entitled to trace any of its resin supplied after the 14 February 1977, the title to which had not passed to S.T.P. under clause 2 of the contract, into any chipboard manufactured from such resin or into the proceeds of sale of such chipboard, but so that Borden could not recover a sum in excess of the contract price of such resin.
(3)　the exercise of the tracing remedy was not a charge created by the company to which section 95 of the Companies Act, 1948, had any application.

With respect, in the view of the present author, the judge was entirely right in all points.

8.06　The *Bond Worth* case

Before the Court of Appeal could deliver judgment in the appeal on the *Borden* case, judgment was delivered by Mr Justice Slade in the *Bond Worth* case on 12 February 1979. His judgment was in the possession of the Court of Appeal when they did come to decide the appeal.

Mr Justice Slade's judgment is extremely long and it is therefore proposed here to summarise the arguments and his conclusions. It has already been noted that it contained implied, and in the judgment of the present author, unwarranted criticism of the judgment of the Court of Appeal in the *Romalpa* case.

8.07   The retention clause

This was in the form of a letter purporting to vary the existing conditions on which goods were supplied. The text has already been printed in full in [2.03].

The clauses are by no means conventional retention of title clauses. By (a) it would appear the legal title to the goods passes to the buyers, but 'equitable and beneficial ownership' was to remain with the sellers.

In short, it was not a retention of title clause at all. Title was to pass to purchaser and the sellers were to be left with equitable ownership.

8.08   The facts of *Bond Worth*

The form of the action was an application to the court for direction by joint receivers appointed by the Alliance Assurance Co. Ltd under trust deeds which created floating charges over the assets as security for debenture stocks in carpet manufacturers, Bond Worth Ltd. Earlier, another receiver had been appointed by the National Westminster Bank. There is no reference to the fact that the position of a receiver is not the same as that of a liquidator [6.15] and the point, it would appear, was not taken, as it was before Judge Rubin [8.04].

Acrilan fibre had been supplied by the first respondents, Monsanto Ltd to Bond Worth Ltd for several years but from 1976 all such supplies had been made under a standard contract of sale to which reference has already been made [2.03]. The clause reserved the equitable and beneficial ownership of Acrilan fibre supplied by Monsanto to Bond Worth until all outstanding indebtedness of Bond Worth to Monsanto had been discharged. The clause further provided that if before payment was made in full, the Acrilan fibre was used in the manufacture of carpets and they were then sold by Bond Worth, Monsanto's equitable and beneficial interest in the fibre would extend to the proceeds of sale.

The National Westminster Bank's receiver went into possession on 16 August 1977. At that date there was owed to Monsanto, for Acrilan delivered to Bond Worth or one of its subsidiaries for which Bond Worth was liable, the sum of £587,397 in respect of twenty-nine deliveries of Acrilan. These, the judge held, were separate contracts of sale in which the property passed to Bond Worth on delivery.

Although no accurate stock appears to have been taken by the receiver, there appears to have been in the possession of Bond Worth:

> £110,000 of unprocessed Acrilan
> £282,000 of yarn made 99.26% from Acrilan
> £163,000 finished carpet stock in which the Acrilan yarn, dyed, formed the substantial part, apart from the latex backing, a total of £555,000 of Monsanto's goods.

The bank's receiver was told by telex on the day of his appointment that all Acrilan on Bond Worth's premises was subject to a retention of title clause.

8.09   The hiving-down operation

The business of Bond Worth Ltd was hived down by the receiver, with effect from the close of business on 16 August 1977, to another company, Glixcroft Ltd. No actual stocktaking of Bond Worth's assets was made by the first receiver appointed by the National Westminster Bank on that day.

The hiving-down agreement was made on 19 August 1977 between that receiver on behalf of Bond Worth Ltd, whereby Bond Worth agreed to sell and Glixcroft agreed to purchase as at, and with effect from, the close of business on 16 August 1977, and free from all liens and charges and incumbrances, the goodwill, undertaking and all other property and assets of Bond Worth, except for a number of stated categories.

Amongst the categories so excluded were 'goods supplied to the vendor under retention of title'.

Mr Justice Slade said: 'The Acrilan which had been delivered to Bond Worth by Monsanto before Mr Milnes' receivership, and which was at the date of his appointment in various stages of manufacture, was used by Glixcroft after that date in the manufacture of carpets.'

He also added:

'Believing it was not legally possible to sell to Glixcroft goods which were subject to retention of title, Mr Milnes stated in the course of a meeting [with Monsanto Ltd] that he would transfer to Glixcroft all goods used in the business excluding those subject to retention of title.'

The judge was asked by the summons to decide the question as to whether, and if so when, Glixcroft Ltd acquired title to the £555,000 worth of Acrilan, in various forms, on the premises of Bond Worth. He regarded that question as irrelevant in the light of his findings, but others may regard it as extremely relevant. Even if Bond Worth Ltd had legal title in those goods, how and when did Glixcroft Ltd acquire title if the receiver had expressly excluded from the transfer to that company any goods subject to a retention of title clause, or what he thought was a retention of title clause? The question as to the validity of the clause is not one of law but of the identity of property acquired by the new company. There was no specific sale or assignment to Glixcroft of ascertained goods. What goods were then transferred to them?

On 27 August 1977, the receiver appointed by the National Westminster Bank was surplanted by two receivers appointed by the debenture holders, Alliance Assurance Company Ltd. Mr Justice Slade said:

'There was not and never has been any entry or other reference in the books of Bond Worth to stocks of Acrilan or goods made from Acrilan withheld from the sale of assets under the hive-down agreement and remaining in the possession, control or disposition of Bond Worth.

'Furthermore no such stocks of goods existed physically, in the sense that there were no Acrilan or goods made from Acrilan separately marked, stored or otherwise set apart from the other assets of Bond Worth, which were sold to Glixcroft.

'The Acrilan and Acrilan-derived products so transferred to Glixcroft were all used and disposed of by Glixcroft in the normal course of its business, being the continuation of the business previously carried on by Bond Worth.'

8.10   The issues

The summons of the two receivers appointed under the debenture deeds raised seven questions of law, in the view of the judge:

(1)   By what manner and at what dates were the twenty-nine relevant contracts respectively concluded?

(2)   Had the retention of title clause been incorporated in such contracts?

(3)   If so, was the clause capable of having any, and if so what, legal effect?

(4)   If the clause was capable of having legal effect, was it registrable under section 95 of the Companies Act, 1948?

(5)   Had there been transferred to Glixcroft, either by virtue of the hive-down agreement or otherwise, any interest in the Acrilan held by Bond Worth at 19 August 1977 and falling within any of the categories referred to in paragraph 2 of the summons?

(6)   On the assumption that the retention of the title clause had been incorporated in the twenty-nine contracts and was capable of having legal effect, but was not registrable, what remedies (if any) should be afforded to Monsanto?

(7)   On the same assumption, was Monsanto's claim entitled to priority over either or both of the floating charges of the Alliance Assurance Company and the National Westminster Bank?

His decisions on (1) and (2) have already been dealt with in [2.03].

8.11   The legal effect of the clause

Mr Justice Slade decided that all the contracts were contracts for the sale of goods within section 1 (2) of the Sale of Goods Act, 1893. He held

'The legal title or property in the Acrilan fibre comprised in any one of the contracts passed to Bond Worth when the fibre was delivered to Bond Worth (see section 18, rule 1, of the Sale of Goods Act, 1893). In using the term 'property' in this context I refer to the general property in the goods, which is the definition given to the word in section 62 (1) of that Act and not merely a special property, such as that possessed by a bailee.'

Rule 1 of section 18 of the Sale of Goods Act, 1893, has been quoted already in [4.07].

His lordship also held that the risk in the goods likewise passed to Bond Worth on delivery, as a result not only of section 20 of the Sale of Goods Act, 1893, but also because of the words of the clause of the contract.

As to the meaning of 'equitable and beneficial ownership', his lordship said,

'... it was manifestly not the intention to confer on or reserve to Monsanto all the rights which would normally be enjoyed by a *sui juris* person, having the sole beneficial title to property, as against the trustee holding the legal title. Mr Sears, on behalf of Monsanto, expressly conceded and affirmed that Monsanto would not, by virtue of its so-called "equitable and beneficial ownership", have had the right to call for re-delivery of the goods, at any rate so long as Bond Worth was not in default under its payments. Bond Worth, on the other hand, was to have far-reaching rights even before payment to deal with the goods, which would not normally be possessed by a trustee holding the legal title therein on behalf of one sole *sui juris* beneficiary.'

In short, the retention of 'equitable and beneficial ownership' did not mean that there was a situation where a trustee is under an obligation to hold the legal title exclusively for the benefit of a beneficiary.

Bond Worth were to be entitled to use the goods for the purpose of manufacture. The parties intended that if the Acrilan became converted into other products, the equitable and beneficial ownership should attach to those products. If Bond Worth were to sell those products, Monsanto's ownership would attach to the proceeds of the sale.

'The real difficulty [said the judge,] arises concerning the meaning and legal effect (if any), of the provisions in the retention of title clause concerning "equitable and beneficial ownership".'

Later he said:

'I readily accept that the court is not entitled to discard the plain ordinary meaning of the phrase "equitable and beneficial ownership" unless there can be found in the relevant contracts other language and stipulations which necessarily deprive it of its ordinary meaning.'

His conclusion was:

'If the clause operated so as to give any legally enforceable rights at all to Monsanto, such rights must necessarily have been rights by way of mortgage or charge.'

And later:

'The technical difference between a 'mortgage' or 'charge', though in practice the phrases are often used interchangeably, is that a mortgage involves a conveyance of property subject to a right of redemption, whereas a charge conveys nothing and merely gives the chargees certain rights over the property as security for the loan (see Megarry and Wade's *Law of Real Property,* 4th edition, at p.887). Technically, therefore, it seems to me the rights (if any) of Monsanto under the retention of title clause fall to be regarded as rights by way of charge rather than mortgage, if it is proper to regard such rights as being no more than rights by way of security. This particular technical distinction, however, is of no practical significance in the present case, since the expression "charge" in the context of section 95 of the Companies Act, 1948, is defined by section 95 as including "mortgage".'

Having satisfied himself that it was no more than an equitable charge, his lordship then went on to hold that it was a charge created not by Monsanto but by Bond Worth.

'I conclude that the proper manner of construing the retention of title clause, together with all the other relevant provisions of the contracts of sale read as a whole, is to regard them as effecting a sale in which the entire property in the Acrilan passes to Bond Worth followed by a security, *eo instanti,* given back by Bond Worth to the vendor, Monsanto.'

And later:

> 'In my judgment, therefore, Bond Worth rather than Monsanto must be regarded as creator of the relevant charges in relation to the ... charged assets.'

His lordship then went on to hold that the charges were therefore ones which should have been registered under section 95 of the Companies Act, 1948, and had not, and were therefore void against any creditor of Bond Worth.

These are contentions that merit close examination; they can best be discussed in a series of questions.

8.12 Can there be equitable ownership of goods?

Lord Atkin suggested *obiter* in *re Wait* (1927) that one of the effects of the Sale of Goods Act, 1893, was to destroy any possibility that there could be equitable, as distinct from legal, ownership of goods.

> 'The rules for transfer of property as between seller and buyer ... appear to be complete and exclusive statement of the legal relations both in law and equity.'

That suggestion has been universally disapproved.

As Lord Hailsham L.C. said in *National Carriers Ltd* v. *Panalpina (Northern) Ltd* (1980), there is no fundamental distinction between real property and personal property. 'There is no difference between chattels and real property except in degree.'

If there can be equitable ownership of real estate there can be equitable ownership of personal property including chattels. That is abundantly clear from cases such as that mentioned above, *re Wait* (1927), in which it was held that ownership passed to a buyer where future goods came to be sufficiently designated as to become specific or ascertained on acquisition by the seller.

> 'A man can contract to assign property which is to come into existence in the future and, when it has come into existence, equity ... fastens upon that property, and the contract to assign becomes a complete assignment. That equity cannot, of course, stop the legal owner selling to anybody else but equity which

fastened upon the title will likewise fasten upon the proceeds of sale.'

It is also a matter of common sense. If Jane provides Tom with the money to buy a motor car which, with her consent, he registers in his own name, and there is no presumption of a gift, she becomes the equitable owner of the car. There is no difference between that situation and the resulting trust which would result from the similar provision of money for the purchase of reality.

When an equitable ownership does arise not as a resulting trust, as it may, but by express contract between the parties or by express declaration, it is a question of construction of the agreement or declaration as to how the legal owner is entitled to deal with the goods. Certainly, he may be entitled to possession and use of them as an attribute of legal ownership. Yet his use can be conditional on terms, and whether or not he can dispose of them depends entirely upon the terms of the agreement or declaration: *re Anchor Line (Henderson Brothers) Ltd* (1936).

Of course, if the legal owner of goods that are subject to equitable ownership disposes of them without the authority of the owner, he may well be able to give a good title to the purchaser under section 25 (2) of the Sale of Goods Act, 1893, or section 25 (1) of the Sale of Goods Act 1979, or the 'estoppel' section 21, of both Acts. In that event equity will fasten upon the proceeds of sale.

But Mr Justice Slade treated the fact that the true owner had no right to call for the redelivery of the goods, so long as Bond Worth was not in default, and that the latter had the right to use them in a manufacturing process, subject to express conditions, as decisive. With respect, it by no means follows.

8.13   Can there be bailment with equitable ownership?
Mr Justice Slade dismissed in one sentence the possibility that there could be a bailment of goods where the legal owner was in possession of them with the consent of the equitable owner. He said:

'There is no question of a bailor-bailee relationship, since it is common ground that the property in the Acrilan fibre passed to Bond Worth at the latest when it was delivered, while it is of the essence of a bailment that the general property in the goods concerned remains in the bailor, while only a special property passes to the bailee, which entitles him to exercise certain "possessory remedies".'

With respect, that is by no means conclusive. There must be a position in equity analogous to the legal bailor/bailee situation, where the possessor of the goods, notwithstanding he has legal title, has all the duties of bailee to the true owner. 'Equity looks to the intent, not the form.' The legal owner of a chattel in possession is under the same duty in equity to preserve the chattel for the true, equitable owner. Can it be said that Tom who has bought the motor car with Jane's money is under no obligation to her in his use of it? So that if he wantonly destroys it, she has no redress?

8.14 Can there be a charge by way of security?
In dealing with the question as to whether the clause which reserved beneficial and equitable ownership to Monsanto was a charge by way of security, Mr Justice Slade said:

'In my judgment, any contract which, by way of security for payment of a debt, confers an interest in property defeasible or destructible upon payment of such a debt, or appropriates such property for the discharge of the debt, must necessarily be regarded as creating a mortgage or charge, as the case may be.'

This sentence is the hinge of the whole of the judgment. It is also, it is submitted, the fundamental fallacy in it.

Mr Justice Slade does not there limit this view of the law to the cases where legal title passed to the purchaser but equitable ownership remained with the supplier. In his view, *any* contract which confers an interest in property, whether legal or equitable, which is defeasible or destructible on the payment of a debt, must *necessarily* be regarded as creating a mortgage or charge. By 'necessarily', of course, his lordship means by operation of law.

That is precisely the argument which was advanced in the House of Lords in *McEntire and Maconchy* v. *Crossley Brothers Ltd* (1895) eighty-five years earlier and decisively rejected by the House of Lords [1.06].

The argument there, advanced by counsel for the appelants, was summarised in the Law Reports:

'The transaction is not one of hiring but of sale and mortgage by the purchaser. The mortgage, being of a chattel, is a bill of sale and, not being registered, is void under the Bills of Sale Acts... . The Court will look to the essence and not merely the form of the agreement. Courts have found no difficulty in construing instruments in a manner contrary to the expressed intention in order to give effect to the real intention. What the parties sought to establish was the relation of seller and purchaser, the former to have a charge on the chattel for the unpaid purchase-money. But, as the charge is not registered ... it is invalid.'

Legal title in that case was reserved but Mr Justice Slade might well have adopted those words as a summary of his own findings for his lordship, in the quotation above, did not differentiate between legal title and 'beneficial and equitable' ownership.

In *re Bond Worth Ltd* the parties had clearly expressed the intention that the real ownership should remain with the sellers and should transfer to any goods made from their Acrilan. There is no reason in law why that contractual obligation should not have been given effect to; still less is there any reason why, in equity, the sellers' rights should be defeated. In justice, too, it is unreasonable that secured creditors should be entitled to seize the property of other persons in order to satisfy their claims; while these persons, the beneficial and equitable owners, are relegated to a 'nil' dividend as unsecured creditors. If that is equity as conceived by the present Chancery Division of the High Court, it would be preferable to have equity determined by the length of the Lord Chancellor's foot.

8.15   The savings of the Sale of Goods Act, 1893

What counsel failed to draw to Mr Justice Slade's attention were the provisions contained in section 61 (4) of the Sale of Goods Act, 1893:

'The provisions of this Act relating to contracts of sale do not apply to any transaction in the form of a contract of sale which is intended to operate by way of mortgage, pledge, charge or other security.'

His lordship held that the terms of the contract of sale between Monsanto Ltd and Bond Worth Ltd were in fact intended to operate by way of a charge. It would appear to follow that, since the terms of 'the form of a contract of sale' were not subject to the provisions of the Sale of Goods Act, 1893, no title to the goods in law was in fact passed to Bond Worth Ltd: *Maas* v. *Pepper* (1905); *The Orteric* (1920). It must follow that the goods in law as well as in equity remained the property of Monsanto Ltd. His findings that the transaction as a whole must be construed as the creation of a charge by Bond Worth vitiates his earlier finding that it was a sale. The two are incompatible.

8.16   The practical effects of *re Bond Worth Ltd*
It is evident from this case that it is not currently expedient to use a retention of title clause which relies solely upon 'beneficial and equitable' ownership. An additional practical effect was to create doubts about the rulings of the unanimous Court of Appeal in the *Romalpa* case.

8.17   Were S.T.P. bailees of the goods?
It was after the *Bond Worth* case that the Court of Appeal heard the appeal in the *Borden* case. The judges in the Court of Appeal had been supplied with copies of that judgment, although it had not as then been published in any law report. It is evident that they were impressed by it.

One of the findings of Judge Rubin had been that Borden had no proprietary interest at common law in any chipboard manufactured by S.T.P. using the resin supplied by Borden. There was no cross appeal against this finding.

The exact words of the order made by Judge Rubin which was being appealed were:

'This court doth declare that the plaintiffs are entitled to trace any of their resin supplied after 14 February 1977, the title to which had not passed to the defendants, Scottish Timber Products Limited under clause 2 of the plaintiffs' standard conditions in the pleadings mentioned, into any chipboard manufactured from such resin or into the proceeds of sale of such chipboard but so that the plaintiffs cannot recover a sum in excess of the contract price of such resin. And this court doth declare that the exercise of such a tracing remedy is not a charge created by the company to which section 95 of the Companies Act, 1948, has any application.'

Lord Justice Bridge, who delivered the first judgment, said:

'... the first question which arises for our decision is whether there was a fiduciary relationship here between S.T.P. and Borden in the nature of the relationship of bailee and bailor.
    '... it is common ground that S.T.P. were at liberty to use the resin which had not been paid for in the manufacture of chipboard, so that before the resin was paid for, the result was that it ceased to exist as such.
    'Is that consistent with the relationship of the parties being that of bailor and bailee?'

His lordship referred to the case of *South Australian Insurance Co.* v. *Randell & Ano.* (1869), the Privy Council appeal case mentioned by Mr Justice Slade, and in particular to an observation of Sir Joseph Napier:

'A bailment on trust implies that there is reserved to the bailor the right to claim a redelivery of the property deposited in bailment.
    'Chancellor Kent in his commentaries ... where he refers to the case of *Seymour* v. *Brown,* of which he disapproves in common with Mr Justice Story, adopts the test, whether the identical subject matter was to be restored either as it stood or in an altered form; or whether a different thing was to be given for it as an equivalent; for in the latter case it was a sale, and not a bailment. This is the true and settled doctrine according to his opinion.'

Accepting that as an accurate expression of the law, Lord Justice Bridges then went on to hold that since the resin was not to be returned in the ordinary course of business, there was no bailment. The other judges did not express an opinion on the point.

8.18   The conditions of bailment

It is pertinent to note that there is in fact no obligation on a bailee to restore the identical subject matter to the bailee 'either as it stood or in an altered form'. A bailee's obligation is to dispose of the goods in accordance with the instructions of the bailor and a person can be a bailee of goods who is agent for the owner to sell them, or to use for his own purposes pending the time when he becomes the owner, as in the ordinary consumer conditional sale or hire purchase agreement.

8.19   Admixture of chattels

Counsel for *Borden* apparently made a concession which was wrong in law and fatal to his case.

Lord Justice Bridge described it thus:

> 'I am quite content to assume ... that up to the moment when resin was used in manufacture, it was held by S.T.P. in trust for Borden in the same sense in which a bailee or a factor or an agent holds goods in trust for his bailor or his principal.
>
> 'If that was the position, then there is no doubt that as soon as the resin was used in the manufacturing process it ceased to exist as resin and accordingly the title to the resin simply disappeared.
>
> 'So much is accepted by [counsel] for the respondent, Borden.'

With respect, it should be said that chattels do not simply disappear because they are admixed with other chattels. Nor is the title to them extinguished by admixture. As Mr Justice Blackburn said in *Buckley* v. *Gross:*

> 'Probably the legal effect of such a mixture would be to make the owners tenants in common in equal portions of the mass, but at all events they do not lose their property in it.'

English law may have few cases, compared to Roman law, on the effect of admixture and all of them deal with accidental admixture. What cases there are do not in any way support the proposition that the identity of chattels admixed with other chattels 'simply disappears': *Spence* v. *Union Marine* (1869); *Sinclair* v. *Brougham* (1914); (see also Holdsworth: *History of English Law*, vol. VII, p. 502).

If goods with a title retained to the seller are sold and the proceeds can be traced into monies, why not into other goods with which they have been admixed, as Judge Rubin held?

As Lord Justice Bridge said:

'Counsel [for Borden] ... argued that "the tracing remedy arises from the mixture of Borden's resin with S.T.P.'s other materials in the manufacture of chipboard, so that an appropriate proportion of the chipboard now represents Borden's security for monies due to them as the unpaid price of all the resin delivered."

'In my judgment, the crux of the whole case is whether this argument can be sustained.'

His lordship continued:

'It is conceded that there is no previous authority which establishes that the tracing remedy can be exercised where there has been an admixture of the goods of A with the goods of B in such a way that they both lose their identity and result in the production of goods of an entirely different kind.'

His lordship held there was no such tracing remedy and distinguished the *Romalpa* case for three reasons:

'First, it was conceded throughout in that case that the defendants were bailees of the aluminium foil for the plaintiffs.

'Secondly, on the facts on which the decision turns, there had been no admixture of the foil with any other material; if there had been, it would have been covered by the express terms of the second part of condition 13, but all that was in issue was a claim to trace the foil into the proceeds of sale of the foil.

'Thirdly, the clause turned on the construction of the particular clause and on what was to be implied in the first part of the clause as to the terms on which the defendants were entitled to sell aluminium foil.'

8.20 The moral of *Borden*

The substance of this judgment therefore is that there do not arise, by operation of law or equity, tracing rights into other chattels by the legal owner of goods. That is a decision which will no doubt have to be looked at by the Court of Appeal if the occasion arises, or by the House of Lords, to see whether it is consistent with *Romalpa* and with the English decisions about the admixture of goods.

But it in no way excludes express contractual provisions giving an unpaid seller legal rights to admixed goods.

As Lord Justice Bridge said:

'The lesson to be learned from these conclusions is a simple one. If a seller of goods to a manufacturer, who knows that his goods are to be used in the manufacturing process before they are paid for, wishes to reserve to himself an effective security for the payment of the price, he cannot rely on a simple reservation of title clause such as that relied upon by Borden.

'If he wishes to acquire rights over the finished product, he can only do so by express contractual stipulation.'

In other words the supplier must write in an aggregation clause.

8.21 The effect of these decisions

The result of the three English decisions on the effect of retention of title clauses is that a seller who reserves the legal title to the goods he sells on delivery of them to a buyer is fully protected and retains priority over the other creditors of the buyer, both as regards his interest in the goods and the proceeds of re-sale. But the present position of the seller who retains only the equitable beneficial title to the goods and the proceeds of re-sale is that he has merely an equitable charge, which will have priority over the claims of other creditors of the buyer only it if is properly protected by registration under the Bills of Sale Acts, 1878 and 1882, or the Companies Act,1948, whichever is applicable; that is, if *Bond Worth Ltd* is followed.

It is, however, unlikely that any future case of the type will come to court since the draftsmen of retention clauses will in future prudently avoid retaining only the equitable and beneficial title.

Chapter 9

French, German and United States' Law

by Professor Robert R. Pennington

9.01 Retention of title clauses overseas

Retention of title clauses are used in contracts for the sale of goods in practically all the commercially developed countries of the world, and in this chapter the relevant law of three of those countries, France, Germany and the United States will be examined.

The laws of most other developed countries follow the pattern set either by the civil law systems of France and Germany, or by the common law system of the United Kingdom or the statutory codification found in the United States.

Additionally, certain countries which basically regulate retention of title arrangements by the general principles of contracts and property law (as do the United Kingdom, France and Germany) have imposed special registration requirements in respect of contracts of sale containing retention of title clauses similar to the requirements of the codified law of the USA.

9.02 Current account provisions: France and Germany

The general law governing the sale and transfer of title to goods in France and Germany is contained in the respective Civil Codes of those countries as interpreted by the courts.

In French law an ordinary contract of sale operates to pass the ownership of the goods to the buyer when the contract is entered into (French Civil Code, arts. 1138 and 1583), but if the goods are not identified and ascertained when the contract is made, ownership does not pass until the seller appropriates particular goods to the contract with or without the assent of the seller.

Under German law the ownership of goods passes to the buyer under a contract of sale only when the goods are delivered to him, but if the goods are in the possession of a third person, the seller may alternatively transfer ownership by transferring his right to call for delivery to the buyer (German Civil Code, paras. 929 and 931).

Under both systems of law it is possible for the seller to retain the ownership of the goods until the price has been paid or until some other condition has been fulfilled, and ownership passes to the buyer only when that has been done (French Civil Code, art. 1181; German Civil Code, para. 158).

The German Supreme Court has expressly recognised the validity of 'current account' provisions in retention of title clauses, even though the ownership of the goods in question may not pass to the buyer before he re-sells or consumes them because the buyer (or another company in the same group if the buyer is a company) may remain continuously indebted to the seller (or other companies in the seller's group) up to that time. Although the French courts have not expressly pronounced on this point, the prevailing view is that current account provisions are effective under French law too.

9.03 The passing of title to goods: USA

United States' law governing contracts for the sale of goods is now uniform in all fifty states, and is set out in the Uniform Commercial Code, which has been adopted by all the state legislatures.

Under an ordinary contract of sale, in the absence of any contrary agreement, the ownership of the goods passes to the buyer when the contract is entered into if the goods are existing and identified at that time; in any other case ownership passes when the goods are physically delivered to the buyer, but the parties may agree that ownership shall pass at the earlier time when the seller appropriates goods to the contract by shipping, marking or otherwise designating them accordingly (Uniform Commercial Code (UCC), art. 2−401 and 2−501 (1)).

The parties may by agreement make the passing of ownership conditional on the occurrence of any event, but as soon as the goods are shipped or delivered to the buyer the ownership of them automatically passes to him, and any retention of ownership by the seller agreed upon by the parties thereupon terminates.

The seller's interest in the goods then becomes a security interest in them, and the seller is treated as though he had taken a mortgage or charge on the goods to secure the price remaining unpaid, or if the parties so agree,the fulfilment of any other condition, such as the discharge of all the buyer's outstanding indebtedness to the seller (UCC, art. 2–401 (1)): *Fidelity and Casualty Co. of New York* v. *Jeffries* (1976). It will be readily seen that the law relating to contracts of sale incorporating retention of title clauses is different in certain basic respects in the United Kingdom, France, Germany and the United States.

This chapter now goes on to examine further differences between them in respect of the nature of the buyer's interest in the goods; the effect of dispositions of the goods by the buyer before he has paid the price and any additional amounts which a retention of title clause is designed to secure; the effect of a retention of title clause extending the seller's rights to the proceeds of re-sale of the goods by the buyer; and the position of the seller in the buyer's insolvency.

9.04   The nature of the buyer's interest

Under the sale of goods where the seller reserves ownership until the price or other amount owing from the buyer is paid (known in French as *réservation de propriété* and in German as *Eigentumsvorbehalt*), the buyer initially acquires only personal contractual rights against the seller, and these ripen into ownership of the goods protected against all third persons only when the buyer pays the price or otherwise satisfies his obligations to the seller and so fulfils the condition on which ownership is to pass, or in United States' law if the goods are previously delivered to him.

In French law, as in English law, this distinction between the buyer's contractual rights and his acquisition of ownership is fully maintained without any overlap. Consequently, until the condition for the transfer of ownership is fulfilled, the buyer has merely what English lawyers would call a 'chose in action' (*droit de créance*), and since the ownership of the goods remains vested in the seller, the risk of loss or damage is borne by him until the price or other amount owing is paid in full and ownership passes to the buyer (French Civil Code, arts. 1138 and 1624): *Denis* v. *Compain* (1906).

Nevertheless, the parties may expressly agree otherwise, and the risk of loss may be placed on the buyer and persons claiming under him from the moment the goods are delivered to him, or even from an earlier time: *Raffenstein* v. *Navarre* (1904).

9.05   The buyer's interest in German law

German law has inclined increasingly over the past fifty years towards treating the rights of the buyer under a sale reserving ownership to the seller (*Eigentumsvorbehalt*) as themselves amounting almost to ownership, and certainly as amounting to more than mere contractual rights against the seller.

In 1933 the German Supreme Court stated that 'the conditional right of the buyer should be regarded as an interest in ownership in expectancy (*Anwartschaftsrecht*) or as a vested right to ownership in the future.' ((1933) RGZ 140 223 225.)

In more recent cases the Germany Supreme Court has ruled that 'The buyer's right to acquire ownership has the character of ownership itself,' and 'the right of the buyer is an anticipatory right of ownership, which is no different in kind from ownership, but is merely ownership in a reduced form.' ((1958) BGHZ 28, 16, 21; (1956) BGHZ 20, 88, 99.)

On the other hand, the German Supreme Court has held that the buyer has no immediate proprietary interest which is an incumbrance of the ownership of the seller, and for that reason it has held that an attempted disposition of the ownership of the goods by the buyer before he had paid for them was governed by the provisions of the Civil Code relating to dispositions by non-owners ((1953) BGHZ 10 69 72.)

The dilemma in which the German courts find themselves is the result of the Civil Code recognising only one category of ownership, namely legal ownership, and ruling out the possibility of a parallel beneficial ownership vested in someone other than the legal owner.

The German courts have sought to give the buyer under reservation of ownership something more than personal contractual rights against the seller, yet something less than full ownership. They have consequently given the buyer's rights a hybrid status which is not recognised by the Civil Code, and in effect they have treated the buyer as already being the owner of the goods in cases where the ownership of the seller does not affect the outcome, and have treated the buyer as the holder of mere contractual rights in cases where the seller's ownership is material.

For example, it has long been held that the risk of loss or damage to the goods passes to the buyer on delivery of the goods to him, and that as from that time he has an insurable interest in them ((1914) RGZ 85 320; (1918) RGZ 93 330; (1910) RGZ 74 126). Furthermore, it has been held that the buyer may sue third persons who wrongfully damage or misappropriate the goods in his possession, and may recover the same damages from them as though he were already the owner of the goods ((1942) RGZ 170 1; (1959) BGHZ 30 375).

On the other hand, the German Supreme Court has implicity held that the buyer does not have real ownership until he pays the amount owing to the seller in a case where the buyer created a mortgage or charge over the goods (or rather over his interest in them) and then sold his interest to a purchaser who was unaware of the charge, but who on later discovering the charge took a transfer of ownership by paying the balance owing to the seller, which, as the court held, operated to free the goods from the charge without vesting them even for a moment in the buyer, and since the ownership was not incumbered by the charge while vested in the seller, it remained unincumbered when the purchaser acquired it ((1956) 3 BGHZ 2088).

If the ownership or something akin to it had been vested in the buyer all along, and payment of the balance owing to the seller had merely perfected the buyer's ownership and made it unconditional, the purchaser would, of course, have acquired ownership through the buyer, and would have taken it, subject to the charge which the buyer had created.

9.06 The buyer's interest in United States' law

United States, law is, of course, far simpler than either French or German law in defining the buyer's interest under a contract of sale which contains a retention of title clause. The buyer obtains full legal ownership of the goods at the latest when they are shipped or delivered to him, and this gives him the full rights of an owner against the seller and third parties: *Meinhard Commercial Corporation* v. *Hargo Woolen Mills Inc.* (1973).

The unpaid seller's interest is simply a charge incumbering the buyer's legal ownership, and the seller's rights are with few exceptions the same as those of any other creditor who has taken a mortgage of the goods to secure what is owed to him.

Nevertheless, the risk of loss of the goods passes to the buyer when the goods are delivered to him or to a carrier for transportation to him (UCC, art. 2–509 (1) and (3)). Furthermore, the buyer has an insurable interest in the goods as soon as they are identified or appropriated to the contract, even though at that time neither ownership nor possession of the goods has passed to him (UCC, art. 2–501 (1)).

9.07   Disposal of the goods by the buyer

The fact that under a contract of sale which reserves ownership to the seller the buyer is normally in possession of the goods from the time the contract is entered into or shortly thereafter, gives him an appearance of already being the owner of the goods which he may use to mislead third persons into dealing with him as owner.

In English law such third persons are generally unprotected against claims by the true owner (i.e. the seller) notwithstanding their good faith and the fact that they give value, but an exception is made in the case of a person who purchases or lends on the security of goods if the buyer has obtained possession of the goods or of documents of title to them with the seller's consent, provided that the third person takes delivery of the goods or documents of title from the buyer in good faith and has no notice of any rights of the seller in respect of the goods (Sale of Goods Act 1979, section 25 (1)): *Lee* v. *Butler* (1893); *Helby* v. *Matthews* (1895).

French and German law similarly protect a third person who deals in good faith with the buyer believing him to be the owner of the goods, but this is not the result of a special exception to the rule that a person who acquires goods cannot obtain a better title to them than the person from whom he acquires them, but is the consequence of the general principle of French and German law that if a person obtains possession in good faith under a pretended transfer or disposal of the ownership of goods by a non-owner, he acquires a valid independent title which extinguishes or overrides the title of the former owner (French Civil Code, art. 2279 (1); German Civil Code, para. 932 (1)).

This rule applies whether the third person takes a pretended full transfer of ownership (as on a sale) or whether he takes a disposal conferring a continuous right to possession coupled with the right to acquire ownership.

Consequently, it has been held by both the French and German Supreme Courts that if the buyer of goods subject to the reservation of ownership to the seller re-sells them to a bona fide purchaser reserving ownership to the buyer until the re-sale price is paid, the purchaser obtains a valid title against the unpaid seller ((1953) BGHZ 10 69): *Remps* v. *Andriot* (1866); *Grunfelder* v. *Genot* (1915).

9.08 Protection of a sub-purchaser

For the purchaser or other third person to be protected under French and German law, however, it is essential that he should obtain possession of the goods, and that he should believe the buyer to be their owner when he does so.

Under French law the delivery to the third person of a document of title to the goods (such as a bill of lading or a consignment note, or a warehouse warrant) is not sufficient for this purpose, unless the purchaser also obtains physical possession of the goods, or at least an acknowledgment from the person who has physical possession of them that he holds the goods at the purchaser's disposition: *Société d'Eclairage d'électricité* v. *Mousset* (1921).

On the other hand, in German law the transfer to a purchaser or other third person of the buyer's right to require delivery of the goods from the person who has physical possession of them does give the purchaser or third person sufficient indirect possession to vest a valid title in him if he is then in good faith, even though before obtaining physical possession of the goods he discovers that the buyer was not their owner; and this is also the case if the purchaser or third person obtains possession of negotiable documents of title to the goods issued or procured by the seller (German Civil Code, para. 934; German Commercial Code, paras. 424, 450 and 650).

The burden of proving good faith on the part of a third person who takes a disposition from a non-owner rests on the third person himself once the plaintiff has established his title, and he will not have acted in good faith if he either knew or suspected that the title of the buyer tð the goods was conditional or otherwise defective, or if he was grossly negligent in not discovering that this was so.

Consequently both the French and German Supreme Courts have held that if in the trade in question it is common practice for goods to be sold subject to the retention of ownership by the seller, a third person who purchases them from the buyer does not act in good faith if he makes no inquiries about the buyer's title or if his inquiries are superficial, and this is particularly so if the third person deals in goods of the kind in question and does not merely acquire them for personal use (German Civil Code, para. 936 (2); (1933) RGZ 143 16): *Desourtheau* v. *Morel* (1965).

9.09   Sub-purchaser in United States' law

United States' law also protects a purchaser of goods from a buyer who has possession of them under a contract of sale reserving the ownership of the goods to the seller, but it does so in a different way from English, French or German law because the seller's interest in the goods is no longer ownership, but merely a security interest like a mortgage or charge.

If the purchaser acquires the goods from the buyer in the ordinary course of the buyer's business, he becomes the owner of the goods free from the interest of the unpaid seller, even if he knows of it (UCC, para. 9–307 (1)).

However, a sale is not in the ordinary course of the buyer's business if it is a bulk sale of his stock in trade, whether in connection with the sale of his whole business to the purchaser or not (UCC, para. 1–201 (9)).

Consequently, it was held that where a seller sold his stock in trade as part of a sale of his retail business to the buyer subject to retention of ownership by the seller until the purchase price was paid, and the buyer in the course of carrying on the business he had acquired sold some of the stock to a purchaser, who was aware of the retention of ownership arrangement with the seller, the purchaser obtained no title to the stock, because the relevant sale was not the sale to him (which was in the ordinary course of the buyer's business) but the sale to the buyer, which, being a bulk sale, was: *National Shawmut Bank of Boston* v. *Jones* (1967).

If the goods sold subject to retention of ownership are consumer goods acquired by the buyer for his personal, household or family use, and the buyer re-sells them to a purchaser who buys them for his own personal, household or family use, the purchaser acquires the ownership of the goods free from any interest of the unpaid seller, unless he is aware of that interest (UCC, paras. 9–109 (1) and 307 (2)). However, the unpaid seller may 'perfect' his security interest in such a case by filing particulars of the contract between himself and the buyer at the appropriate state registration office, although he is not obliged to do this (UCC, paras. 9–204 (1), 302 (1) and 303 (1)).

If the seller has filed a financing statement containing such particulars, a consumer-purchaser will acquire the goods subject to the unpaid seller's security interest, unless the seller has authorised the buyer to re-sell them, e.g. by the retention of title clause in the contract between the seller and the buyer extending to the proceeds of a re-sale by the buyer (UCC, paras. 9–306 (2) and 307 (2)).

9.10 The unpaid seller's right to the proceeds of re-sale

If the contract of sale reserving the ownership of goods to the unpaid seller extends his rights to the proceeds of re-sale by the buyer, under English law the seller has the right to claim the proceeds as his own property, since the buyer is considered to have re-sold the goods as an agent for the seller and he holds the proceeds of re-sale as a fiduciary for the seller.

By contrast, the express reservation to the seller of the right to receive the re-sale price operates as an assignment of it in French and German law, and this is so even if the buyer is expressed to be an agent of the seller in effecting the re-sale or a fiduciary for the seller of the proceeds of re-sale.

In German law such a reservation of the right to the proceeds of re-sale can be made by the original contract of sale, or by the seller's general business conditions which the buyer accepts as the basis for successive purchases from the seller; the assignment takes effect from the moment a contract for re-sale is entered into, when the purchaser is contractually committed to pay the price agreed with the buyer (German Civil Code, para. 398; (1931) RGZ 133 234; (1932) 136 100). All that is necessary is that it should be possible to identify with certainty the amounts payable to the buyer which the seller will be entitled to claim under the assignment.

However, if the reservation of the ownership of goods by the original contract of sale continues until all indebtedness of the buyer to the seller is discharged, there should be a provision in the original contract of sale to ensure that the amount currently owing to the seller bears a reasonable relationship to the value of the goods and their proceeds of re-sale which are reserved to the seller. If the value of the goods and proceeds reserved is excessive, the seller may be held to have acted in bad faith in disregard of the interests of the buyer's other creditors, and the whole reservation of title may then be held void.

However, in the case decided by the German Supreme Court where this was held to be the law, the reservation was held valid because it was expressly provided that if it would at any time extend to goods and re-sale prices worth more in total than 120 per cent of the buyer's current indebtedness to the seller, the excess value in goods most recently supplied or in re-sale prices most recently contracted would not be reserved to the seller ((1952) BGHZ 7 365).

Since the reservation to the seller of the right to the re-sale price operates as an assignment, it is fully effective against the purchaser on the re-sale as soon as it is known to him, and this may result from either the buyer or the seller informing him of it (German Civil Code, para. 407 (1)).

The purchaser cannot then set off against the seller's claim any debt which the buyer owes the purchaser and which has not fallen due before the purchaser becomes aware of the assignment, but the purchaser may rely on any other defence which he could raise against the buyer under the contract for re-sale; e.g. error, fraud, misdescription of the goods, failure by the buyer to fulfil the contract of re-sale (German Civil Code, paras. 404 and 406).

9.11   The unpaid seller in French law

In French law the reservation of the re-sale price to the seller by the original contract of sale raises the problem whether a debt or chose in action arising under a contract entered into after the date of an attempted assignment can be validly assigned at all.

Normally the contract for the re-sale of the goods is entered into by the buyer after the original contract of sale containing the retention of title clause, and at the time that contract is made the debt for the re-sale price payable by the purchaser does not exist.

In some of its decisions, the French Supreme Court has held that future debts and choses in action may be assigned and the arrangement takes effect when they come into existence, whilst in other cases the Supreme Court has held that an assignment of a right is valid only if the contract under which it arises was entered into before the assignment is made.

The prevailing opinion among legal writers is that debts and rights which may arise under future contracts should be fully assignable, since there is no prohibition on this in the Civil Code, and the only legal requirement should be that the assignment identifies the rights with sufficient certainty for them to be immediately recognisable as falling within the scope of the assignment when they do arise.

If this more liberal view is correct, the reservation to the seller of the right to receive the proceeds of re-sale of goods by the buyer would be effective if contained in the original contract of sale or in the seller's general business conditions.

If the stricter view represents the law, however, there seems to be no reason why an attempted advance assignment of re-sale prices should not be effective as a contract by the buyer to assign the right to receive the price when he does in fact re-sell the goods, in which case all that is necessary to make the assignment effective is for the buyer to confirm the agreement when the contract for re-sale has been entered into.

9.12 Retention of title and charges over book debts in common law

When a seller couples the reservation of the ownership of goods with a reservation of the right to the price on re-sale by a buyer who is a manufacturer or a dealer, a competition for priority may occur if the buyer also charges the book debts owing from customers of his business (including debts owing to him from the sale or re-sale of goods) to a bank or financial institution in order to secure an advance.

In German law a general assignment of present and future debts made by the buyer (e.g. to secure a fluctuation overdraft) is valid in principle for the same reasons as a general reservation of the re-sale price of goods to an unpaid seller, and is subject to the same rules.

The only legal requirement is that the future debts to be comprised in the assignment by way of security (*Sicherungsabtretung*) should be defined with sufficient clarity in the instrument of assignment so that no difficulty will arise in determining whether they are within it or not ((1937) RGZ 155 26; (1952) BGHZ 7 365; (1958) BGHZ 27 306).

Difficulties therefore arise when a bank or financial institution makes advances to a manufacturer or trader on the security of a general or global assignment of his future trade or book debts, and he then buys goods from his suppliers subject to the reservation of the ownership of the goods and the proceeds of re-sale to the seller.

The German Supreme Court has held that the normal rule is that the competing claims of the lender and the seller to the re-sale price rank in the chronological order in which they are created ((1957) BGHZ 26 178; (1960) BGHZ 32 361), and this usually gives the bank or financial institution priority because its contract with the buyer precedes the contract between the seller and the buyer.

An assignee of a debt should give the debtor notice of his assignment so that the debtor may not discharge his liability by making payment to the original creditor or a later assignee (German Civil Code, paras. 407 and 408). But the order in which notice is given does not govern priorities between the assignees themselves. Consequently, the seller, who is likely to learn of the re-sale of the goods he supplied to the buyer before the buyer's bank, cannot gain priority over it by being the first to notify his claim to purchasers from the buyer, and even if he obtains payment of the re-sale price from a purchaser so as to discharge him from liability, the seller is still accountable to the bank for what he has received.

There are, however, two exceptional cases where the seller's claim to the proceeds of re-sale are preferred.

The first is where at the time the bank or financial institution takes its global assignment of the buyer's book debts, it knows that the buyer, or manufacturers or traders in his area of business activity, ordinarily acquire goods subject to retention of owner-ship by the seller until the price is paid, and it seems unnecessary that the bank or institution should also know that the sellers also usually reserve the proceeds of re-sale by the buyer as well, if in fact they do ((1959) BGHZ 30 149; (1960) BGHZ 66 384).

The reason for the seller being preferred to the bank in this situation is that so long as the buyer does not re-sell the goods, the seller's reservation of ownership gives him a security which obviously prevails against the bank, even if the buyer becomes bankrupt.

It would be unfair for the bank to be able to claim priority over the seller merely because the goods have been re-sold, when the bank must have realised from the beginning that the buyer's sup-pliers were likely to look to the proceeds of re-sale of the goods as the source from which they would be paid.

The other situation in which an earlier global assignment of book debts to the bank will be postponed to the later reservation of the proceeds of sale to the seller, is where the bank has taken such extensive security over the buyer's trading assets (including book debts) that it must have realised that there was a serious risk of the buyer not having sufficient free assets to satisfy his other creditors, or at least a serious risk that he would contract extensive debts to persons believing him to be the unincumbered owner of the assets charged to the bank and who would allow him credit accordingly ((1932) RGZ 136 247).

The bank is postponed in this case because of its lack of good faith in taking too extensive a security.

9.13   Retention of title and charges over book debts in French law
French law governing the assignment or charging of book debts has not developed as extensively as German law, and the French courts have not often been called on to resolve conflicting claims for priority when the book debts charged as security for a bank loan include the re-sale price of goods sold subject to the reserva-tion of the re-sale price to the seller.

One of the reasons for this is that in recent years banks have increasingly financed current trading by subrogation arrangements, under which they pay the book debts owed to undertakings (less discount, commission, etc.) and then collect the debts themselves (*subrogation conventionelle*).

A subrogation agreement merely substitutes the bank for the buyer who is owed the re-sale price of goods which he has re-sold to his customers but, of course, the subrogated bank has no better claim to the re-sale price than the buyer whom it finances (French Civil Code, art. 1250 (1)).

It is not surprising, therefore, that there is no developed case law in this area, and that the only rule which can be employed to resolve conflicting claims is the provision in the Civil Code that an assignment, mortgage or pledge of a debt or chose in action (*créances*) is effective against the debtor and third parties only when the assignment, mortgage or pledge has been formally notified to the debtor by a notice served by a bailiff (*huissier*) (French Civil Code, arts. 1690 and 2075).

In other words, a seller who has reserved the re-sale price on the sale of goods, and a bank which makes advances to the buyer on the security of the re-sale price, rank for repayment out of the proceeds of re-sale in the order in which they have respectively served formal notices of their interests on the purchaser from the buyer: *Mourreton* v. *Blanco* (1849).

If the bank is merely subrogated to the buyer's right to recover the re-sale price, however, it can serve no such formal notice, and is in any case as much subject to the rights of the unpaid seller as the buyer himself. The result is that the unpaid seller whose reserved rights extend to the proceeds of re-sale of the goods is always preferred to the bank.

9.14 Retention of title and charges over book debts in United States' law

United States' law is more explicit with regard to the rights of an unpaid seller who has retained the ownership of goods to claim the proceeds of their re-sale by the buyer.

If the contract of sale is silent as to the seller's right to claim the proceeds of re-sale, it is implied that his security interest in the goods extends to the proceeds, unless the contract contains provisions inconsistent with this (UCC, arts. 9–203 (3) and 306 (2)).

If the contract of sale expressly extends the seller's rights to the goods and their 'proceeds', this includes all proceeds of re-sale, whether re-sale is for cash or on credit terms (UCC, art. 9–306 (1)).

If the contract expressly authorises the buyer to re-sell the goods, the unpaid seller's security extends to the proceeds of sale by implication, and this includes the benefit of the contract of re-sale if it reserves the ownership of the goods to the buyer until the purchaser has paid the re-sale price: *Commercial Credit Corpn. v. National Credit Corpn.* (1971).

Proceeds of re-sale which have been paid to the buyer can also be claimed by a seller who is entitled to 'proceeds', and if the buyer has paid them into his bank account which is overdrawn or if he later draws out so much from his bank account that the credit balance is less than the proceeds paid into it, the seller can claim the whole of those proceeds from the bank unless the seller's security interest is ineffective against the bank under the rules next considered: *Associates Discount Corporation* v. *Fidelity Union Trust Co.* (1970); *Universal C.I.T. Credit Corpn.* v. *Farmers' Bank of Portageville* (1973).

9.15 USA: registrable financing statement
Normally the unpaid seller's security interest in the proceeds of re-sale is treated as continuously perfected (and so is enforceable against third persons) if the seller's original security over the goods has been perfected (UCC, art. 9—306 (3)).

However, it will be recalled that if the seller's security is for the unpaid price of consumer goods sold for the buyer's personal, family or household use, it is not necessary that a financing statement should have been filed at the state registration office for this purpose (UCC, art. 9—306 (3)). In that case if a financing statement has not been filed in respect of the retention of title to the goods, the seller must file a financing statement relating to the proceeds of re-sale he seeks to recover not later than ten days after the buyer receives them (UCC, art. 9—306 (3)). If the seller does not do this, his security over the proceeds of re-sale ceases to be enforceable against third persons (UCC, art. 9—301 (1)).

Whatever the nature of the goods or the capacity in which the buyer purchases them, conflicting security interests in the goods and the proceeds of their re-sale generally rank for priority in accordance with the order in which financing statements are filed in respect of them at the state registration office (UCC, arts. 301 (1), and 312 (5) and (6)).

But there are important exceptions to this rule when the seller's security is for the unpaid price of the goods. In respect of both the goods themselves and the proceeds of their re-sale, the unpaid seller can claim to have the price owing to him satisfied before the claims of any other secured creditor of the buyer who has already filed a financing statement to protect his own security interest, provided that the seller both files a financing statement and notifies the other secured creditor of the seller's interest before delivering the goods to the buyer (UCC, art. 9–312 (3)). Alternatively, the unpaid seller may preserve his right to payment of the unpaid price out of the proceeds of re-sale in priority to any other secured creditor of the buyer by filing a financing statement not later than ten days after the buyer receives the proceeds of re-sale (UCC, art. 9–312 (4)).

9.16   USA: current account provisions

It will be noted that the exceptions to the normal rule in favour of an unpaid seller apply only insofar as he claims priority for payment of the unpaid price of the goods in question out of the proceeds of sale of the goods.

If the retention of title clause in the original contract of sale contains a 'current account' provision so that the seller has a security interest to secure additionally all other amounts owing to him (or to companies in the same group) from the buyer (and companies in the same group), the general rule applies that priority between competing secured creditors is determined by the order in which they respectively file financing statements (UCC, art. 9–312 (5) and (6)).

Consequently, in the common situation where a manufacturing or dealing company is financed generally by a bank which takes a general charge over the company's book debts or accounts receivable owing from its customers from time to time and files a financing statement accordingly, a seller who later supplies goods to the company on retention of title terms incorporating a 'current account' provision may, on taking the necessary steps of filing and notifying the bank, recover the unpaid price of the goods supplied out of the respective proceeds of re-sale before the bank's claim is satisfied, but the seller cannot treat the global indebtedness of the buyer to him as a single claim payable out of the global proceeds of re-sale if this would prejudice the bank's claim.

On the other hand, the seller may do this if he enters into a master agreement with the buyer governing all future supplies of goods and containing a 'current account' provision; the arrangement will then be effective against the bank if the seller files a financing statement before the bank does so: *Holzman* v. *L.H.J. Enterprises Inc.* (1973).

9.17 Insolvency, bankruptcy and liquidations

The most difficult problems in connection with the sale of goods subject to the retention of ownership to the seller arise when the buyer becomes insolvent and is either made the subject of bankruptcy or insolvency proceedings or, in the case of a company, goes into liquidation. The rules of law discussed above apply in these events, of course, but they may be modified by the special rules governing bankruptcies or liquidations which apply in these circumstances.

Under French, German and United States' law, whilst insolvent companies may be made bankrupt, the liquidation of a company in no way alters its rights and liabilities to third persons, and since such companies either cannot or do not create floating charges over the whole of their assets, receiverships are unknown.

Consequently, only the bankruptcy of a French, German or United States business undertaking which buys goods subject to the reservation of ownership calls for consideration here.

The basic principles of French, German and United States' bankruptcy law are the same as those of English law, and only the few relevant differences between the three systems need be noted here.

In the first place the bankrupt's assets are not transmitted in the trustee in bankruptcy (*syndic; Konkursverwalter*), but remain vested in the bankrupt subject to the trustee's exclusive power to dispose of them and to enforce claims by the bankrupt against third persons (Law No. 67–563 of 13 July 1967, art. 15 (France); *Konkursordnung* of 1877, para. 15 (Germany); US Code, Title 11 (Bankruptcy) paras. 323, 541 and 542 (United States)).

Secondly, a trustee in bankruptcy under French or German law has no power to disclaim the bankrupt's property or contracts. Under United States' law a trustee in bankruptcy may with the court's approval abandon any property comprised in the bankrupt's estate, including contracts he has entered into (US Code, Title 11, para. 554). The consequences are similar to those of disclaimer by a trustee under English law. Thirdly, in French, German and United States' law there are no statutory provisions by which goods in the reputed ownership of the bankrupt may be treated as his assets, but decisions of the French courts have produced much the same effect in the case of sales of goods reserving ownership to the seller.

9.18   Bankruptcy of the buyer
French, German and United States' law differ substantially in their treatment of the rights of the parties if the buyer becomes bankrupt subject to retention of ownership by the seller.

Nevertheless, under all these systems the buyer's trustee in bankruptcy can pay or tender the balance owing to the seller, and thereupon the legal ownership of the goods vests in the buyer as part of his assets administered by the trustee (Law No. 67−563, art. 38 (1) (France): *Konkursordnung,* para. 17 (1); *Smith* v. *Hill* (1963) (United States)).

It is when the buyer's trustee repudiates the contract of sale that French, German and United States' law differ in their treatment of the seller's rights.

9.19   Bankruptcy of the buyer: German law
Under German law an unpaid seller may terminate the contract of sale if the buyer's trustee does not elect to perform it, and he may then recover the goods *in specie* out of the buyer's assets (*Konkursordnung,* para. 43); or if the buyer has disposed of them without the seller's authority, the seller may recover the value of the goods out of the buyer's assets in priority to all his other creditors (*Konkursordnung,* para. 46).

In this latter case the law assumes that the buyer has obtained a re-sale price equal to the value of the goods, and that his assets have consequently been unjustly increased to that extent. In allowing the seller to recover the value of the goods out of the buyer's assets, the law therefore does not prejudice his general creditors, since his assets are merely reduced to what they would have been if he had not made the unauthorised disposal. The seller cannot recover the value of the goods in this way if he authorised or consented to the disposal, however (German Supreme Court (1926)

RGZ 115 262; (1958) BGHZ 27 306). If he consented to the disposal but did not reserve the right to the re-sale price to himself, he cannot claim it in the buyer's bankruptcy, either out of the buyer's assets if it has been paid to the buyer, or from the purchaser on the re-sale if it has not (German Supreme Court (1931) RGZ 133 40).

9.20 Bankruptcy of the buyer: French law

In contrast to German law and subject to one exception, French law does not permit an unpaid seller to recover goods delivered to the buyer under the contract of sale, unless he. has taken steps to do so before the buyer is adjudged bankrupt.

This is because the buyer's possession of the goods may have encouraged his general creditors to advance or extend credit to him on the assumption that he was their legal owner.

The rule is a strict one, however, and it is not possible for the seller to avoid its application by proving that no creditor of the buyer has in fact been misled.

The rule has been established by several decision of the French Supreme Court, which have held that the seller must be treated in the same way as a seller under a contract of sale which transfers ownership of the goods to the buyer immediately, but contains a condition revesting the ownership of the goods in the seller in the event of the buyer's failure to pay: *Société des automobiles Berliet* v. *Renard* (1934); *Vernay* v. *Société Française des Sucreteries* (1935); *S. A. d'Etirage de Soissons* v. *Mannesmann Export GmbH* (1975).

This invokes the provisions of the bankruptcy legislation which prevent the seller from recovering the goods *in specie,* unless he has notified the buyer that the contract of sale is terminated and has demanded the return of the goods before the buyer is adjudged bankrupt. If the seller has done either of these things, it is immaterial that he obtains judgment for the recovery of the goods after the adjudication (Law No. 67–536, art. 61). It is not sufficient for the seller merely to have demanded payment of the price or alternatively the return of the goods by the buyer, however, nor for him to have retaken possession of the goods without notifying the buyer that the contract of sale is terminated: *General Motors Finance Co.* v. *Coccoz* (1938); *S.A. Vêtements Tebra* v. *Ferrari* (1969).

The one exception to the rule that the seller cannot recover the goods unless he has terminated the contract of sale before the buyer is adjudged bankrupt is where the seller's retention of the ownership of the goods is embodied in a written contract or declaration by the seller made before the goods are delivered to the buyer which specified the goods sufficiently clearly to enable them to be identified (Law No. 80–335 of 12 May 1980, art. 1).

In this case, as in the situation where the seller has already notified the buyer of the termination of the contract of sale, the seller may recover the goods *in specie* from the buyer's trustee in bankruptcy provided he sues the trustee within four months after the buyer's adjudication (Law No. 80–335, art. 2).

If the buyer has re-sold the goods without the seller's authority, however, the seller has no claim to the re-sale price, whether it has been paid to the buyer or his trustee in bankruptcy or not: *Touvay* v. *S.A. de dépôt et agence de vente d'usines métallurgiques* (1938); *Touvay* v. *Polbo* (1946).

Formerly, if the seller could have recovered the goods themselves out of the buyer's assets (i.e. because he terminated the contract of sale before the buyer's adjudication), he had a special statutory right to the re-sale price and could recover it either from the buyer's trustee in bankruptcy if it had been paid, or from the purchaser on the re-sale if it had not (Law No. 67–563, art. 66).

This right has now been abolished, however (Law No. 80–335, art. 4).

The seller may now only recover the value of the goods if they are sold without the seller's permission by the buyer's trustee in bankruptcy (and not by the buyer), when the seller will be able to recover their value as an expense or liability incurred in the bankruptcy proceedings: *Hourdant-Blanc* v. *Pellegrino frères* (1907).

If the seller has no right to recover the goods or the proceeds of their re-sale, he ranks merely as an ordinary creditor for the price in the buyer's bankruptcy: *Marmies* v. *Campillo* (1948); *Benazeth* v. *Etabissements Bablot* (1960).

9.21 Problems in German law

The reservation to the seller of the right to the re-sale price of goods also gives rise to problems in French and German law if the buyer becomes bankrupt. In German law the reservation operates as an immediate transfer of the right to the re-sale price to the seller when the buyer enters into the contract for re-sale, but the transfer is only by way of security for the unpaid price on the original sale to the buyer or such other amounts as the reservation of ownership of the goods to the seller was intended to cover.

Consequently, in the buyer's bankruptcy the reservation of the re-sale price is treated as though it were a pledge or a charge on the re-sale price given by the buyer (German Supreme Court (1927) RGZ 118 209); so the seller is entitled to recover the re-sale price from the purchaser, but can retain out of it only the original price due from the buyer or such other amount as was covered by the reservation of the ownership of the goods (*Konkursordnung,* paras. 48 and 127).

If the purchaser has paid the re-sale price to the buyer, either because the seller authorised him to receive it or because the purchaser has not been notified that the seller is entitled to it, the purchaser cannot, of course, be compelled to pay the re-sale price a second time to the seller. The re-sale price will now simply be a sum of money mixed with the buyer's other assets, and the seller cannot compel the buyer's trustee in bankruptcy to pay him an equivalent amount out of those assets, or claim any priority for his claim as a creditor of the buyer (German Supreme Court (1918) RGZ 94 194). Consequently, in this situation the seller loses the benefit of his security for the amount owing to him, and must claim simply as an unsecured creditor for the same dividend as the buyer's other creditors.

Normally, the time at which the buyer re-sells the goods is immaterial in determining the validity of the seller's claim to the proceeds of re-sale in the buyer's bankruptcy.

There is, however, a provision in the German bankruptcy legislation which may affect the seller's claim if the buyer re-sells after ceasing to pay his debts in the ordinary course of his business, or after a bankruptcy petition has been presented against him.

This provision invalidates pledges, charges or other securities created by a debtor over any of his assets after that time, if the secured creditor is aware that the debtor has ceased to pay his debts or has a bankruptcy petition pending against him, and he is in fact subsequently adjudged bankrupt (*Konkursordnung,* para. 30 (1)).

When the buyer re-sells goods whose re-sale price has been reserved to the seller, the reservation gives rise at that time to a charge over the re-sale price in favour of the seller, and it was formerly held by the German Supreme Court that if the re-sale took place when the buyer had ceased to pay his debts, the seller lost his charge over the re-sale price if he was then aware of the buyer's financial condition ((1959) BGHZ 30 238).

The German Supreme Court has since reversed this view in so far as the reservation of the re-sale price to the seller secures the payment of the original price owing to the seller ((1975) BGHZ 64 312).

Its reason for doing so is that the statutory provision is designed to prevent the buyer's creditors from being prejudiced by a diminution of his assets on the eve of his bankruptcy, and the switching of the unpaid seller's security for the original price from the goods themselves to the right to recover the re-sale price does not have this effect, since the buyer's assets are not reduced.

The same reasoning would seem to apply if the reservation of ownership covered amounts owing to the seller other than the price of the goods which the buyer has re-sold, but the court declined to extend the seller's exemption beyond the original price of the goods.

9.22   Problems in French law

In French law the reservation to the seller of the right to the price of the goods re-sold by the buyer operates either as an assignment or as an agreement to assign the buyer's rights against the purchaser under the re-sale, and the assignment or agreement attaches to the re-sale price immediately the contract for re-sale is made.

If the re-sale takes place after the buyer has ceased to pay his debts in the ordinary course of his business, the assignment could in principle be made ineffective by either of two provisions of the French bankruptcy legislation on the buyer subsequently being adjudged bankrupt.

The first of these provisions invalidates pledges and charges given by the debtor after ceasing to pay his debts over any of his assets to secure debts previously contracted (Law No. 67–563, art. 29 (2) No.6).

The second provision empowers the court to invalidate dispositions of the debtor's assets made by him after ceasing to pay his debts if the disposee was aware of his financial condition (Law No. 67–563, art. 31).

In practice, neither of these statutory provisions will normally apply to contracts of sale reserving the re-sale price to the seller when the buyer re-sells the goods after ceasing to pay his debts. It has been held by a *Cour d'Appel* that the first provision does not invalidate the substitution of a new security for one created before the debtor ceases payment of his debts if the value of the new security does not exceed that of the former one; *Netto* v. *Vaudouer* (1906); *Credit Industriel de Normandie* v. *Jaillard* (1936). This is usually the situation when the seller reserves the right to the re-sale price of goods in substitution for his former ownership of them.

If the re-sale price obtained by the buyer exceeds the value of the goods supplied by the seller, it is uncertain whether the assignment of the re-sale price to him is valid to the extent of the value of the goods supplied, or whether it is totally void. The latter alternative would seem absurd, since the seller has no control over the amount of the re-sale price obtained by the buyer, and if the goods supplied by the seller are incorporated in a larger product, the re-sale price of that product is bound to be greater than the price of the goods supplied.

The second bankruptcy provision only applies if the assets of the debtor are diminished as a result of the impugned transaction: *Thalmann Frères* v. *Lagelouze* (1900); *Luneau-Nouvellon* v. *Roc* (1902).

On the re-sale of goods supplied under reservation of ownership this is unlikely to be the case, since the value of the buyer's interest in the goods before the re-sale (i.e. their value less the amount owing to the seller which is covered by the reservation of ownership) will not normally exceed his interest in the re-sale price after deducting the amount owing to the seller.

Although under French law the seller appears to be adequately protected even if the buyer re-sells the goods without receiving the re-sale price before being adjudged bankrupt, he is left unprotected as regards his claim to the re-sale price if the buyer has collected it and at the date of his adjudication the money representing it forms part of his general assets.

This is because the buyer's duty to account to the seller is a purely personal one, as it is in German law, and the seller has no proprietary claim to the money paid to the buyer by the purchaser under the re-sale (French Civil Code, art. 1993): *S.A. de dépôt et agence de vente d'usines métallurgiques* (1938).

Formerly an exception to this is made by the bankruptcy legislation itself: if the seller had begun proceedings to terminate the original contract of sale before the buyer was adjudged bankrupt, or if the seller had notified the buyer of his intention to terminate the contract before that time, the seller could recover the amount of the re-sale price out of the buyer's assets in priority to his other creditors, and it was immaterial in this situation whether the buyer sold the goods before or after ceasing to pay his debts (Law No. 67 –563, art. 66). This exception has, however, now been repealed (Law No. 80–335, art. 4).

9.23   Bankruptcy of the buyer: USA

By comparison with French and German law, United States' law governing the position of a seller of goods who has retained the ownership of them until the price is paid, or the buyer's total indebtedness to the seller is discharged, is essentially straightforward in the event of the buyer's bankruptcy.

This is because the unpaid seller's interest in the goods and in the proceeds of their re-sale (if his interest extends to the proceeds) is treated in all respects as though it were a mortgage or charge created by the buyer over property which is already owned by him.

Consequently, the unpaid seller's interest is effective against the buyer's trustee in bankruptcy only if it has been perfected before the presentation of the petition on which the court orders the liquidation of the buyer's assets (UCC, art. 9–301 (1) and (3)).

Normally, the seller's interest is perfected by filing an appropriate financing statement at the state registration office, except in the case of sales of consumer goods, and so, except in that case, the seller must have effected a filing before the presentation of the petition if his rights in respect of the goods and their proceeds are to prevail against the buyer's trustees in bankruptcy.

However, if the seller enters into the contract with the buyer before the presentation of the petition, and files a financing statement at the state registration office within ten days after delivering the goods to the buyer, the seller's security interest is effective against the buyer's trustee in bankruptcy, despite the fact that a bankruptcy petition has meanwhile been presented (UCC, art. 9–301 (2)).

Furthermore, the seller's perfected security interest under a contract made with the buyer before the presentation of a bankruptcy petition against him is effective against the buyer's trustee in bankruptcy not only as regards the goods comprised in the contract, but also as regards the proceeds of their re-sale by the buyer or his trustee after the commencement of the bankruptcy (US Code, Title 11, para. 552 (2)).

9.24   The position of the unpaid seller: USA
The estate of a bankrupt includes all property which he acquires after the commencement of the bankruptcy proceedings by the presentation of a petition and before the termination of the proceedings (US Code, Title 11, β 54 (7)).

Consequently, the ownership of goods sold to a buyer after the commencement of his bankruptcy vests in him as part of his estate, even though the seller has reserved the ownership to himself, until the price is paid, The seller's security interest is valid, however, whether confined to the goods themselves or extending to the proceeds of re-sale, and the buyer's trustee in bankruptcy cannot dispose of the goods or retain the proceeds of their re-sale without satisfying the seller's claim for the unpaid price of those goods in full: *Tower and Combustion Inc.* v. *Wilson* (1962).

It is uncertain in this situation whether the seller needs to perfect his security interest by filing a financing statement before he delivers the goods to the buyer, or within ten days afterwards (UCC, art. 9–301 (2) and (3)).

It would appear, however, that since the trustee in bankruptcy has only as good a title to the goods or their proceeds as the buyer himself, the seller's security interest is binding on the trustee even though it has not been perfected. This view is fortified by the conferment on the unpaid seller of a statutory right to reclaim goods delivered to an insolvent buyer within ten days after delivery if the seller was unaware of the buyer's insolvency at the time, and this right is enforceable against both the buyer and his trustee in bankruptcy (UCC, art. 2–702 (2)): *re Bel Air Carpets Inc.* (1971); *Re Telemart Enterprises Inc.* (1975); cert. denied (1976).

The remedies available to a seller whose security interest under a retention of ownership provision is effective against the buyer's trustee in bankruptcy fall under two heads, namely, the seller's remedies under the contract of sale and his remedies to enforce the security interest vested in him by reason of the retention of ownership provision.

If the goods have already been delivered to the buyer, the seller may under the contract of sale either rescind and cancel the contract so that ownership of the goods revests in the seller, or he may claim the unpaid price as a creditor in the buyer's bankruptcy, but he cannot do both these things (UCC, art. 2–703 (e) and (f)): *Encore Inc.* v. *Olivetti Corporation of America* (1976).

Clearly the seller benefits most by cancelling the contract, because he may then recover the goods themselves instead of merely receiving a dividend out of the buyer's estate as an unsecured creditor.

Recovery of the goods is only possible, of course, if the buyer has not re-sold the goods. If he has re-sold them and in many situations when he has not, the seller will pursue the alternative course of enforcing his security interest as though he were a mortgagee of the goods and (where appropriate) the proceeds of their re-sale by the buyer or his trustee in bankruptcy.

In that case the seller may on the failure of the buyer and his trustee to pay the amount owing, recover possession of the goods if the buyer or his trustee has not re-sold them, and he may also sell the goods and pay off the amount owing out of the proceeds of sale (UCC, art. 9–503 and 504 (1)).

Alternatively, if the buyer or his trustee has re-sold the goods and the seller's security interest extends to the proceeds of re-sale, the seller may recover the re-sale price from the purchaser if the seller notifies him of the seller's claim to receive it before the purchaser pays it to the buyer or his trustee (UCC, art. 9–502 (1)): *Feldman* v. *Philadelphia National Bank* (1976).

If the re-sale price has already been paid to the buyer or his trustee, the seller may recover the proceeds out of the buyer's estate if they can still be identified.

If the proceeds have been paid into a bank account, the seller may recover out of the account the amount of proceeds received by the buyer during the ten days before the commencement of his bankruptcy, less the amount of proceeds paid to the seller during that period and the amount of identifiable proceeds recoverable by the seller (UCC, art. 9–306 (4)).

In effect this gives the seller limited statutory tracing rights similar to the rights conferred by the English rules of equity.

9.25   The chaos of the conflict of laws

The foregoing examination of the laws governing sales of goods subject to retention of title by the seller in three leading commercial countries of the world shows how widely they each differ from English law and from each other.

The relevant law in each country is an amalgam of the rules governing ordinary contracts of sale, of those parts of the law of moveable property which concern the transfer of title to goods and mortgages and charges over goods and debts, and of certain of the statutory rules of bankruptcy and insolvency law.

The mixture is different in each country, and the rules themselves differ widely. It is not surprising therefore that when retention of title clauses are used in connection with international sales, the problems to which they give rise are almost intractable.

Most systems of law accept that a contract with an international element is governed by the system of law which the parties intended (usually the law of the country where the contract is principally to be performed), that the transfer of title to goods and mortgages of goods and debts is governed by the law of the country where the goods are situate or the debt is payable, and that the relevant rules of bankruptcy and insolvency law are those of the country where the bankruptcy or insolvency proceedings are taken.

Unfortunately, these rules of thumb do not often provide a ready solution to the problem in hand, because what one system of laws classifies as a question of contract law another will treat as a question of ownership, and confusion is made worse when rules of equity are introduced which have no equivalent in many foreign systems of law.

So far only half-hearted attempts have been made to bring about a rationalisation and harmonisation of national laws on the retention of title on the sale of goods. Chaos is likely to continue for a substantial time yet.

When eventually a serious attempt is made at international codification, the model most likely to commend itself is the United

States' Uniform Commercial Code, which has the great virtues of directness, relative simplicity and, above all, practicality.

Chapter 10

The Law and the Conduct of Receivers

10.01   A summary of English law

It is now possible to summarise English law in the form of a series of propositions based on the assumption that the law has been correctly expressed in the *ratio decidendi* of the leading cases. The present author does not accept that this assumption is necessarily correct (he has indicated his doubts by the words 'sed dub.'); and he considers that the judgment in *re Bond Worth Ltd* will not be binding on any other high Court judge, and that many of the observations made in *Borden (U.K.) Ltd* v. *Scottish Timber Products Ltd & Ano.* are inconsistent and incompatible with the *Romalpa* case itself. Some day, presumably, unless Parliament intervenes by legislation, a future Court of Appeal will be faced with the attempt to reconcile these two cases and should, if it is to be faithful to English law, prefer *Romalpa.*

Subject to these qualifications, it is submitted that English law currently supports these propositions:

(1)   If an unpaid seller retains the legal title to goods he has agreed to sell, this is a conditional sale within the meaning of section 19 (1) of the Sale of Goods Act 1979 and the property does not pass to the buyer until the buyer has paid the sale price to the seller. (2)   If a purchaser who has not paid for goods subject to a retention of title clause is allowed possession of these goods by the seller, he is the bailee of those goods for the seller, irrespective of whether he is licensed by the seller to sell-on the goods he has

received to a sub-purchaser or whether he is licensed to process those goods or admix or adjoin them to other materials.

(3) The proceeds of re-sale of such goods, provided they can be traced in accordance with the ordinary equity rules for the tracing of trust assets, belong to the unpaid seller in priority to all other claims, whether the buyer is solvent or insolvent.

(4) This right to trace the proceeds of sale does not amount to a charge which is required to be registered under the Bill of Sales Acts or under section 95 of the Companies Act, 1948 for three reasons: first, because it is not in its nature a charge; secondly, because even if it were a charge, it would not be one *created* by the buyer (within the term of section 95) and, in any event, it would be one that came into effect by operation of law and not by the volition of the parties.

(5) That being so, a contractual undertaking whereby the buyer agrees to hold the proceeds of re-sale of the goods for the seller until payment of the full sale price is not itself a charge for the same reasons and for the additional reason that it only expresses in contractual terms the obligations that the law already imposes upon any bailee.

(6) If the buyer with the express or implied licence of the seller processes, mixes or adjoins the seller's goods with those of his own or those of any other person, the seller does not by operation of law become part owner of the product (*sed dub.*).

(7) However, it is open to the buyer to expressly contract with the seller that if he, the buyer, processes, mixes or adjoins the seller's goods with his own or another person's goods, the ensuing product shall be the exclusive property of the seller or, alternatively, that the product so produced shall be owned in common with the seller or with another person.

(8) Thereafter, the buyer becomes the bailee of the product so produced for the unpaid seller.

(9) If such products are sold-on, the proceeds of re-sale are held by the buyer as fiduciary for the unpaid seller in accordance with the rule in *re Hallett*.

(10) The fiduciary obligations thus produced do not constitute a registrable charge under the Sale of Goods Acts or section 95 of the Companies Act, 1948 for the same reasons as are set out in (4) above.

(11) If the buyer contracts to hold the proceeds of re-sale of the product for the unpaid seller until payment of the full sale price, this is likewise not a charge for the reasons set out in (5) above. (12) If equitable ownership alone is reserved and legal title passes to the buyer the effect of this may amount to no more than a floating charge registrable under section 95 of the Companies Act, 1948 (*sed dub.*).

10.02　No part of contract of sale

That being the present position, it may be noted that the actual practice of receivers appointed by banks, or other secured creditors such as debenture holders, is in many respects contrary to it. Their main concern is to exact from the company the maximum of assets for the secured creditor who has appointed them, so long as they do not become personally liable.

Their first line of defence is to raise the objection, as was done in the three leading cases unsuccessfully, that the retention of title clause is not part of the contract of sale (see Chapter 2).

It is therefore imperative that any seller who wishes to rely on a retention clause should ensure that the intending buyer has notice of the terms before the contract is concluded. To print such terms merely on an invoice is insufficient, since the contract is usually concluded before the invoice is prepared.

10.03　Identification of goods

The second line of defence of receivers commonly is to claim that the onus of proof rests on the supplier who has retained title to show that the goods on the premises of the company are his goods and that such goods have not been paid for.

This is a reversal of the common law presumption. A person interferes with the goods of another at his own peril. The onus is on one who sells, or otherwise disposes of goods, to ensure that he has the right to do so, including the power to confer title on a purchaser. Receivers presume that all the goods on a company's premises or in its possession are the company's property. There is no such presumption in law and the statutory doctrine of reputed ownership has no application to companies.

But where a supplier notifies a receiver that he has supplied goods to the company with a reservation of title, the receiver will usually resist the supplier's claim on the grounds that it is for the supplier to produce positive proof that can identify the goods on the company's premises.

With common materials, such as the aluminium foil, resin or Acrilan mentioned in the leading cases, this can be very difficult for the supplier. Even with goods identifiable by unit numbers, it is common practice these days for such numbers not to be quoted on delivery notes or invoices. Moreover, even though goods are acknowledged to be of the supplier's manufacture, a receiver will often resist the supplier's claim on the ground that they could have been supplied from another source, e.g. a wholesaler. A supplier should therefore be careful to identify in his own records or on delivery notes or invoices the goods supplied if they are capable of such identification.

10.04   Proof that goods are not paid for

The next line of defence of the receiver is to require the supplier to prove not merely that his goods are in the company's possession but also that they are not paid for. Where there is a 'current account' clause, if the account has at any time been in credit, the receiver will require the supplier to prove that the goods, reluctantly admitted by the receiver to have been supplied by him, are not those where title has been already transferred by payment to the company. This may be very difficult for the supplier to do.

Even when there is no 'current account' clause, but just a simple retention, there may well be on the company's premises goods which have been paid for, where the title has passed to the buyer, and those which have not yet been paid for, and of which the unpaid seller is still the owner. The receiver will insist that the unpaid seller proves that the goods remaining are his property and, in the absence of proof beyond reasonable doubt, will proceed to treat all the goods as if they were the company's property.

There is, however, a principle of law which ought to be raised against receivers in these situations, although it would appear that this has not yet been done in any retention of title case. There are two maxims of the common law which express the same principle. One is: *omnia praesumtur legitime facta donec probetur in contrarium;* the other is *omnia praesumuntur rite et solemniter esse acta.* 'Everything is presumed to have been legitimately done, unless the contrary is proved' and 'Everything is presumed to have been done in accordance with rectitude and regularly'. The problem, therefore, of the proof of ownership of different parcels of resin or of Acrilan which have been admixed, some of which has been paid for and some of which has not, is really very simple. Although the supplier may not be able to identify what has been paid for from what has not, the law will presume that the buyer was an honourable person who rightly and regularly conducted his business. Such a person would undoubtedly use his own property which he had paid for before he would use somebody else's, for which he had not paid. The presumption therefore follows (unlike the trade union maxim 'first in, last out') that goods that are received earlier will be presumed to have been used earlier, i.e. 'first in, first out'. Thus where there are goods on hand and are unpaid sums, these goods must be assumed to be the property of unpaid seller so far as they do not exceed the unpaid sum.

Evidence of practice to the contrary may, of course, rebut this presumption.

10.05   Access to company's premises

There may be no implied right on the part of unpaid seller to enter on the premises of a company to whom he has supplied goods and retained the title to recover those goods, and it is therefore prudent to write into the contract the express right to do so in the event of a receiver being appointed or a winding-up order made or a resolution for winding-up being passed.

However, notwithstanding such express terms, it is the usual practice of receivers to refuse to allow an unpaid seller on to the premises. As has been pointed out, receivers have no greater powers than the company has and, unlike the company, are not in occupation of the premises [6.03]. The appropriate remedy therefore appears to be an application to the court for a mandatory injunction against the receiver, which can be sought *ex parte*. Since there can be no legal justification for this conduct, it is submitted that this would be an appropriate case for costs being ordered against the receiver, for which he would not be entitled to be indemnified out of the company's assets or by the party appointing him. His obligation as agent for the secured creditor is to comply with the law and with the company's contractual obligations. He can only seek indemnity in so far as he does so.

10.06 Actions against receivers

Receivers appointed by debenture holders or other secured creditors are in no way privileged from actions against them for wrongs committed by them in that capacity. In *Six Arlington Street Investments Ltd* v. *M. J. Spencer* (1979) the receiver appointed by the bankers of a company called Arco (Europe) Ltd was held liable for damage done to the plaintiff's premises by persons the receiver had instructed to remove the company's moveable assets from the leased premises. The task of removing machinery and chattels had been performed in what was described by the trial judge as 'a rough and ready manner, leaving the property in a shambles ... as though the removal had been conducted by a gang of cowboys'. The judge said: 'It was the receiver's duty to give good vacant possession of the premises when they were handed over ... and he is accountable for clearing up the cost of clearing up the sad state of disarray and debris in which ... at least part of the premises were left.'

This case is a salutary reminder that receivers are not above the law and that they are personally liable for the manner in which they handle other peoples' property, real or personal.

10.07 Tactical manoeuvres

The right of a receiver (or liquidator) to apply to the court for directions by way of summons is one that an unpaid seller with a retention clause should try to defeat wherever possible. 'Litigation is not a game of catch-as-catch-can,' said a judge recently. With respect, it is exactly that. Tactical manoeuvering can defeat even the best legal claim, and usually does.

A summons can be taken out and an application made to the court for directions at no risk to the receiver. In any event, his costs will be a first charge on monies received on behalf of the secured creditor; if he is successful in his contentions the unpaid seller will be condemned in the costs of resisting the summons.

An unpaid seller with a retention clause should therefore, as soon as his claim is disputed by a receiver or not acknowledged in full, seek an *ex parte* injunction to restrain the receiver from parting with the goods, pending a settlement of the dispute.

Where the receiver has professed to vest the title to the goods in a hive-down company or to otherwise sell them on, whether as received or as processed in any way, it is important to take out immediately a writ claiming damages for detinue and/or conversion of the goods. For these torts a receiver may be personally liable without recourse to those who appointed him or such assets. There is nothing like the prospect of personal liability to concentrate the mind of a receiver wonderfully. Whereas if the receiver gets to the court first on a summons for directions, he is in a 'heads I win, tails you lose' situation.

When the unpaid seller sues the receiver for detinue or conversion, he has the initiative. Once he has established on a balance of probabilities, including the presumption mentioned above [10.04] that the receiver has been guilty of either tort, the receiver is thrust into the position of having to justify his actions as a matter of law and also has to prove that the company had title to the goods of which he disposed. Moreover, damages are not limited to the mere value of the goods or the price received by the receiver but are any which flow naturally from the wrongful act.

The remedy against a receiver for wrongful detention of goods is a writ demanding delivery up of the goods in question, together with damages for wrongful detention. An order for delivery up can be made under the Order 14 procedure for summary judgment in the High Court. The measure of damages will depend on the purpose for which the goods were intended to be used. There is no universally applicable rule for such damages, it was said in *Brandeis Goldschmidt & Co. Ltd* v. *Western Transport Ltd* (1981); the ordinary standards of damage for tort are applicable.

10.08   Admixed goods

The present practice of receivers is to claim that, as an effect of the *Borden* case, once goods subject to a retention clause are admixed with other goods, the goods cease to exist as chattels. This point has already been discussed [8.21]. It will be gathered that, in that case, there was no specific vesting by the contract of admixed property in the unpaid seller, and the case proceeded on the concession of counsel for Borden that the existence of chattels ceased once admixed. Moreover, all the case decided was that there was not, by operation of law or equity, any title to the product by one whose goods were with his consent admixed with those of another. But, as Lord Justice Bridge pointed out [8.21] in the *Borden* case, if an unpaid seller 'wishes to acquire rights over the finished product, he can do so by express contractual stipulation'.

There is, clearly, no legal objection to making the unpaid seller either the entire owner of the product made from his goods or the part owner. The Sale of Goods Act 1979 contemplates part owner-ship of goods, ownership jointly by one or more person, since section 1 (1) expressly provides:

> 'There may be a contract of sale between one part owner and another.'

A receiver will be as much liable for conversion of goods part owned by another as goods wholly owned.

The suggestion has been made that the creation of rights over manufactured products may constitute a specific charge over goods which has to be registered under section 95 – presumably as a floating charge over part of the company's property. That cannot be so, since the section does not in any way deal with property in goods vested in another.

It was then further suggested that once such goods were sold on or otherwise disposed of, the seller's rights to such goods were automatically converted into a floating charge registrable under section 95. This suggestion is entirely contrary to the principles set out in *Romalpa.* It is most regrettable that any doubt has been cast upon this very clear judgment of the Court of Appeal by the obscurities of subsequent cases.

As has been pointed out [6.10] in a mortgage or charge there is no sale of goods and the transaction is the exact opposite in that it is the mortgagor who transfers the title of his property to the mortgagee in order to secure a debt. A charge is registrable under section 95 as a floating charge only if created a charge over *the company's* property.

If the manufactured goods in question are not the company's property, it cannot be a mortgage or charge.

Neither suggestion therefore will serve as a defence to an action in tort for detinue or conversion or to defeat the tracing rights given by equity in accordance with *re Hallett.*

The cardinal principle of law must not be allowed to be sub-merged by the strategems of receivers: they have no great powers or rights that were vested in the company to which they were appointed receivers [6.14]. A company can never be allowed to set up the claims of debenture holders to defeat the rights of unpaid sellers of goods who have retained title; nor can the debenture holders themselves or their receivers.

10.09   A registrable charge?

Two of the Lord Justices of Appeal in the *Borden* case expressed the view, *obiter,* that an express aggregation clause might amount to a charge registrable under s.95 of the Companies Act 1948. This was never argued before them and was quite irrelevant to the facts of the case. It would appear that the Registrar of Companies does not take this view and refuses to register such clauses. No matter. It is sufficient in order to protect any registrable charge, to deliver the prescribed particular to the Registrar even if he refuses or fails to register the charge: *N.V. Slavenburg's Bank* v. *Intercontinental* (1980). In all cases of 'current account clauses' [3.02], 'proceeds of sale' clauses [3.04], and 'aggregation clauses' [3.05] it may be prudent to send a recorded delivery letter to the Registrar asking for registration and at the same time expressly disclaiming that the clause is registrable as a charge.

but s wld hdd xs for
B if contract subsisted

Donaldson in Clough mill

Draft Retention of Title Clauses

Before drafting any retention of title clause, it is advisable to consider the category set out in [1.11] into which goods to be sold fall.

The following clauses may be applicable:

Category 1: *Goods bought for consumption*
    clauses: A, B, C, E, G, H
    possibly: D, F

Category 2: *Goods bought for re-sale substantially as they are purchased*
    clauses: A, B, C, E, G, H, J(i), M(i)
    possibly: D, F

Category 3: *Goods bought to be incorporated in another chattel substantially as they are purchased*
    clauses: A, B, C, E, G, H, J, K, L, M
    possibly: D, F

Category 4: *Goods bought for the purpose of admixing with other materials and to be processed so as to constitute substantially a new chattel*
    clauses: A, B, C, E, G, H, J, K, L, M
    possibly: D, F

*Category 5: Goods bought with the intention that they shall cease
to exist as chattels*
clauses: A, B, C, D, E, G, H, J(i), L, M(i)
possibly: D, F

The terms of trade of XYZ PLC (hereinafter called 'the Company'):—

All goods are supplied to intending purchasers on the following
terms, and no person in the employment or acting otherwise as
agent of the company or purporting so to do, has authority to
accept orders, supply goods on any other conditions or to vary
these terms in any way whatsoever. Previous dealings between
the company and any customer shall not vary or replace these
terms or be deemed in any circumstances whatsoever so to do.
Acceptance of goods from the company shall be conclusive
evidence before any court or arbitrator that these terms apply.

(A) The intending purchaser acknowledges that before entering
into an agreement for the purchase of any goods from the company
he has expressly represented and warranted that he is not
insolvent and has not committed any act of bankruptcy, or
being a company with limited or unlimited liability, knows of
no circumstances which would entitle any debenture holder or
secured creditor to appoint a receiver, to petition for winding-
up of the company or exercise any other rights over or against
the company's assets.

(B) Goods the subject of any agreement by the company to
sell shall be at the risk of the intending purchaser as soon as
they are delivered by the company to his vehicles or his premises
or otherwise to his order.

(C) Such goods shall remain the sole and absolute property of
the company as legal and equitable owner until such a time as
the intending purchaser shall have paid to the company the
agreed price.

(D) together with the full price of any other goods the subject
of any other contract with the company.

(E) The intending purchaser acknowledges that he is in possession of goods solely as bailee for the company until such time as the full price thereof is paid to the company.

(F) together with the full price of any other goods the subject of any other contract with the company.

(G) Until such a time as the intending purchaser becomes the owner of the goods, he will store them on his premises separately from his own goods or those of any other person and in a manner which makes them readily identifiable as the goods of the company.

(H) The intending purchaser's right to possession of the goods shall cease if he, not being a company, commits an available act of bankruptcy or if he, being a company, does anything or fails to do anything which would entitle a receiver to take possession of any assets or which would entitle any person to present a petition for winding-up. The company may for the purpose of recovery of its goods enter upon any premises where they are stored or where they are reasonably thought to be stored and may repossess the same.

(I) In the case of any purchaser who is not a company, the purchase price shall be payable in two instalments, namely 10% on receipt of the goods and the balance thereof at the end of such time as may be separately agreed or in default of agreement thirty days after the delivery of the goods.

(J) Subject to the terms hereof, the intending purchaser is licensed by the company to process the said goods in such fashion as he may wish and/or incorporate them in or with any other product or products subject to the express condition that the new product or products or any other chattel whatsoever containing any part of the said goods shall be separately stored and marked so as to be identifiable as being made from or with the goods the property of the company.

(K) If goods the property of the company are admixed with goods the property of the intending purchaser or are processed with or incorporated therein, the product thereof shall become and/or shall be deemed to be the sole and exclusive property of the company. If goods the property of the company are admixed with goods the property of any person other than the intending purchaser or are processed with or incorporated therein, the product thereof shall become or shall be deemed to be owned in common with that other person.

(L) The intending purchaser shall be at liberty to agree to sell-on any product produced from or with the company's goods on the express condition that such an agreement to sell shall take place as agents and bailees for the company whether the intending buyer sells on his own account or not and that the entire proceeds therefore are held in trust for the company and are not mingled with any other monies and shall at all times be identifiable as the company's monies.

(M) If the intending purchaser has not received the proceeds of any such sale he will, if called upon so to do by the company, within seven days thereof assign to the company all rights against the person or persons to whom he has supplied any product or chattel made from or with the company's goods.

Alternatives
(J)(i) Subject to the terms hereof the intending purchaser is licensed by the company to agree to sell on the company's goods, subject to the express condition that such an agreement to sell shall take place as agents, save that the intending buyer shall not hold himself out as such, and bailees for the company, whether the intending buyer sells on his own account or not and that the entire proceeds thereof are held in trust for the company and are not mingled with other monies or paid into any overdrawn bank account and shall be at all times identifiable as the company's monies.

(M)(i) If the intending purchaser has not received the proceeds of any such sale, he will if called upon so to do by the company, within seven days thereof assign to the company all rights against the person or persons to whom he has supplied any product or chattel made from or with the company's goods.

The purpose of clause (I), to be used in the case of individuals or partnerships, is set out in [6.05].

Neither the author nor the publishers accept legal liability of any kind in respect of the above suggested draft clauses.

Sales of Goods Act 1979: selected sections

2—(1) A contract of sale of goods is a contract by which the seller transfers or agrees to transfer the property in goods to the buyer for a money consideration, called the price.

(2) There may be a contract of sale between one part owner and another.

(3) A contract of sale may be absolute or conditional.

(4) Where under a contract of sale the property in the goods is transferred from the seller to the buyer the contract is called a sale.

(5) Where under a contract of sale the transfer of the property in the goods is to take place at a future time or subject to some condition later to be fulfilled the contract is called an agreement to sell.

(6) An agreement to sell becomes a sale when the time elapses or the conditions are fulfilled subject to which the property in the goods is to be transferred.

4—(1) Subject to this and any other Act, a contract of sale may be made in writing (either with or without seal), or by word of mouth, or partly in writing and partly by word of mouth, or may be implied from the conduct of the parties.

(2) Nothing in this section affects the law relating to corporations.

5—(1) The goods which form the subject of a contract of sale may be either existing goods, owned or possessed by the seller, or goods to be manufactured or acquired by him after the making of the contract of sale, in this Act called future goods.

(2) There may be a contract for the sale of goods the acquisition of which by the seller depends on a contingency which may or may not happen.

(3) Where by a contract of sale the seller purports to effect a present sale of future goods, the contract operates as an agreement to sell the goods.

6 Where there is a contract for the sale of specific goods, and the goods without the knowledge of the seller have perished at the time when the contract is made, the contract is void.

12—(1) In a contract of sale, other than one to which sub-section (3) below applies, there is an implied condition on the part of the seller that in the case of a sale he has a right to sell the goods, and in the case of an agreement to sell he will have such a right at the time when the property is to pass.

(2) In a contract of sale, other than one which subsection (3) below applies, there is also an implied warranty that—

(a) the goods are free, and will remain free until the time when the property is to pass, from any charge or encumbrance not disclosed or known to the buyer before the contract is made, and

(b) the buyer will enjoy quiet possession of the goods except so far as it may be disturbed by the owner or other person entitled to the benefit of any charge or encumbrance so disclosed or known.

(3) This subsection applies to a contract of sale in the case of which there appears from the contract or is to be inferred from its circumstances an intention that the seller should transfer only such title as he or a third person may have.

(4) In a contract to which subsection (3) above applies there is an implied warranty that all charges or encumbrances known to the seller and not known to the buyer have been disclosed to the buyer before the contract is made.

(5) In a contract to which subsection (3) above applies there is also an implied warranty that none of the following will disturb the buyer's quiet possession of the goods, namely—

(a) the seller;
(b) in a case where the parties to the contract intend that the seller should transfer only such title as a third person may have, that person;
(c) anyone claiming through or under the seller or that third person otherwise than under a charge or encumbrance disclosed or known to the buyer before the contract is made.

16 Where there is a contract for the sale of unascertained goods no property in the goods is transferred to the buyer unless and until the goods are ascertained.

17—(1) Where there is a contract for the sale of specific or ascertained goods the property in them is transferred to the buyer at such time as the parties to the contract intend it to be transferred.

(2) For the purpose of ascertaining the intention of the parties, regard shall be had to the terms of the contract, the conduct of the parties and the circumstances of the case.

18 Unless a different intention appears, the following are rules for ascertaining the intention of the parties as to the time at which the property in the goods is to pass to the buyer.

Rule 1—Where there is an unconditional contract for the sale of specific goods in a deliverable state the property in the goods passes to the buyer when the contract is made, and it is immaterial whether the time of payment or the time of delivery, or both, be postponed.

Rule 2—Where there is a contract for the sale of specific goods and the seller is bound to do something to the goods for the purpose of putting them into a deliverable state, the property does not pass until the thing is done and the buyer has notice that it has been done.

Rule 3—Where there is a contract for the sale of specific goods in a deliverable state but the seller is bound to weigh, measure, test, or do some other act or thing with reference to the goods for the purpose of ascertaining the price, the property does not pass until the act or thing is done and the buyer has notice that it has been done.

Rule 4—When goods are delivered to the buyer on approval or on sale or return or other similar terms the property in the goods passes to the buyer:—

(a) when he signifies his approval or acceptance to the seller or does any other act adopting the transaction;

(b) if he does not signify his approval or acceptance to the seller but retains the goods without giving notice of rejection, then, if a time has been fixed for the return of the goods, on the expiration of that time, and, if no time has been fixed, on the expiration of a reasonable time.

Rule 5—(1) Where there is a contract for the sale of unascertained or future goods by description, and goods of that description and in a deliverable state are unconditionally appropriated to the contract, either by the seller with the assent of the buyer or by the buyer with the assent of the seller, the property in the goods then passes to the buyer; and the assent may be express or implied, and may be given either before or after the appropriation is made.

(2)　Where, in pursuance of the contract, the seller delivers the goods to the buyer or to a carrier or other bailee or custodier (whether named by the buyer or not) for the purpose of transmission to the buyer, and does not reserve the right of disposal, he is to be taken to have unconditionally appropriated the goods to the contract.

19—(1) Where there is a contract for the sale of specific goods or where goods are subsequently appropriated to the contract, the seller may, by the terms of the contract or appropriation, reserve the right of disposal of the goods until certain conditions are fulfilled; and in such a case, notwithstanding the delivery of the goods to the buyer, or to a carrier or other bailee or custodier for the purpose of transmission to the buyer, the property in the goods does not pass to the buyer until the conditions imposed by the seller are fulfilled.

20—(1) Unless otherwise agreed, the goods remain at the seller's risk until the property in them is transferred to the buyer, but when the property in them is transferred to the buyer the goods are at the buyer's risk whether delivery has been made or not....

(3) Nothing in this section affects the duties or liabilities of either seller or buyer as a bailee or custodier of the goods of the other party.

21—(1) Subject to this Act, where goods are sold by a person who is not their owner, and who does not sell them under the authority or with the consent of the owner, the buyer acquires no better title to the goods than the seller had, unless the owner of the goods is by his conduct precluded from denying the seller's authority to sell....

25—(1) Where a person having bought or agreed to buy goods obtains, with the consent of the seller, possession of the goods or the documents of title to the goods, the delivery or transfer by that person, or by a mercantile agent acting for him, of the goods or documents of title, under any sale, pledge, or other disposition thereof, to any person receiving the same in good faith and without notice of any lien or other right of the original seller in respect of the goods, has the same effect as if the person making the delivery or transfer were a mercantile agent in possession of the goods or documents of title with the consent of the owner....

41—(1) Subject to this Act, the unpaid seller of goods who is in possession of them is entitled to retain possession of them until payment or tender of the price in the following cases:—

(a) where the goods have been sold without any stipulation as to credit;
(b) where the goods have been sold on credit but the term of credit has expired;
(c) where the buyer becomes insolvent.

(2)   The seller may exercise his lien or right of retention not-withstanding that he is in possession of the goods as agent or bailee or custodier for the buyer.

61—(1) In this Act, the context or subject matter otherwise requires...

"contract of sale" includes an agreement to sell as well as a sale...

"delivery" means voluntary transfer of possession from one person to another...

"future goods" means goods to be manufactured or acquired by the seller after the making of the contract of sale;

"goods" includes all personal chattels other than things in action and money, and in Scotland all corporeal moveables except money; and in particular "goods" includes emblements, industrial growing crops and things attached to or forming part of the land which are agreed to be severed before sale or under the contract of sale....

"property" means the general property in goods, and not merely a special property...

"sale" includes a bargain and sale as well as a sale and delivery;

"seller" means a person who sells or agrees to sell goods;

"specific goods" means goods identified and agreed on at the time a contract of sale is made....

Table of Cases

Note

The following abbreviations of English Reports are used:

A.C. – Law Reports Appeal Cases Series
All E.R. – All England Law Reports
Ch. – Law Reports Chancery Series
E.R. – English Reports
K.B. – Law Reports King's Bench Series
Q.B. – Law Reports Queen's Bench Series
W.L.R. – Weekly Law Reports

Where other Reports are referred to, their full title is given.
Where foreign cases are cited, the country of origin is indicated.

Table of Statutes

Index